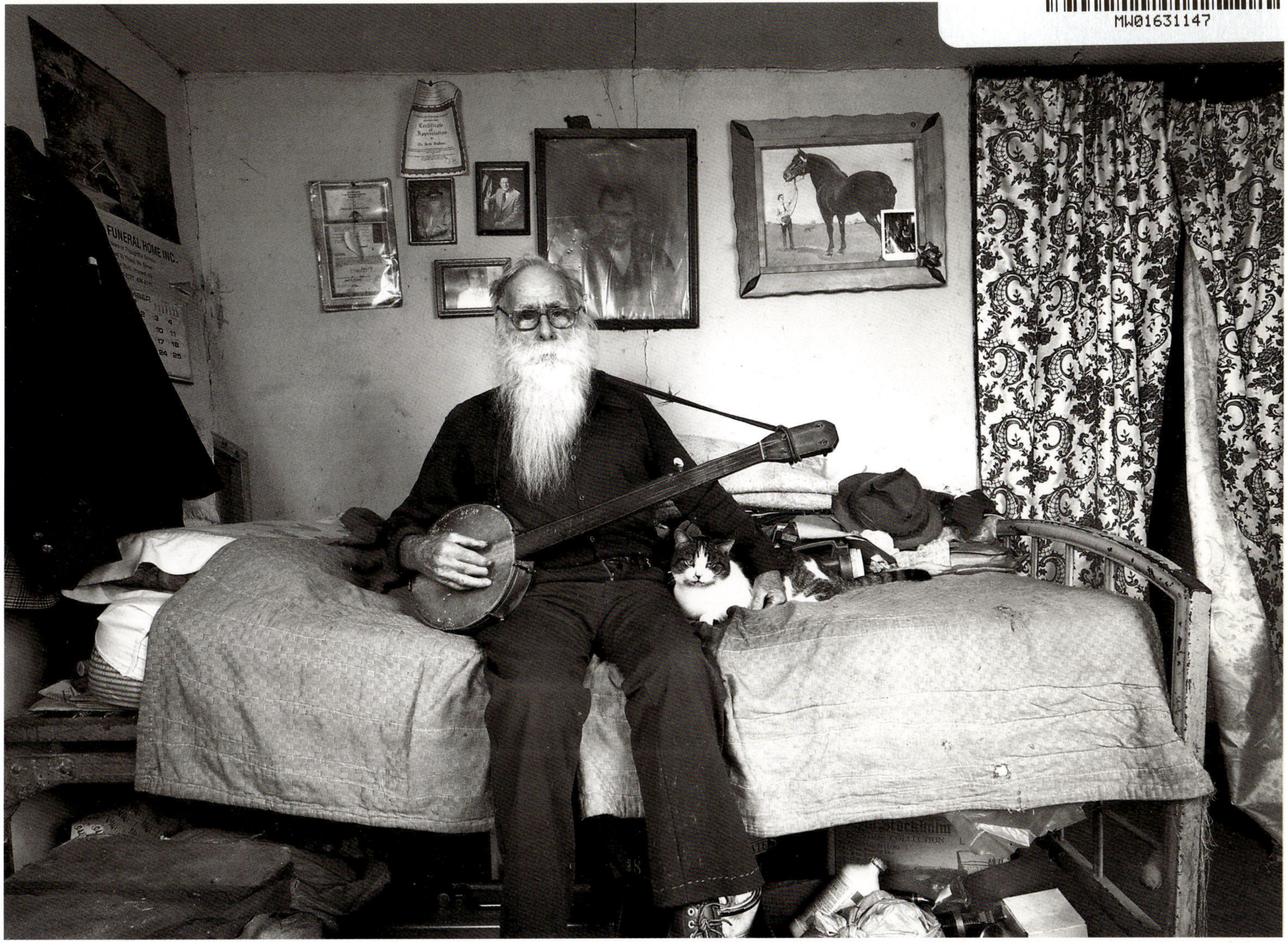

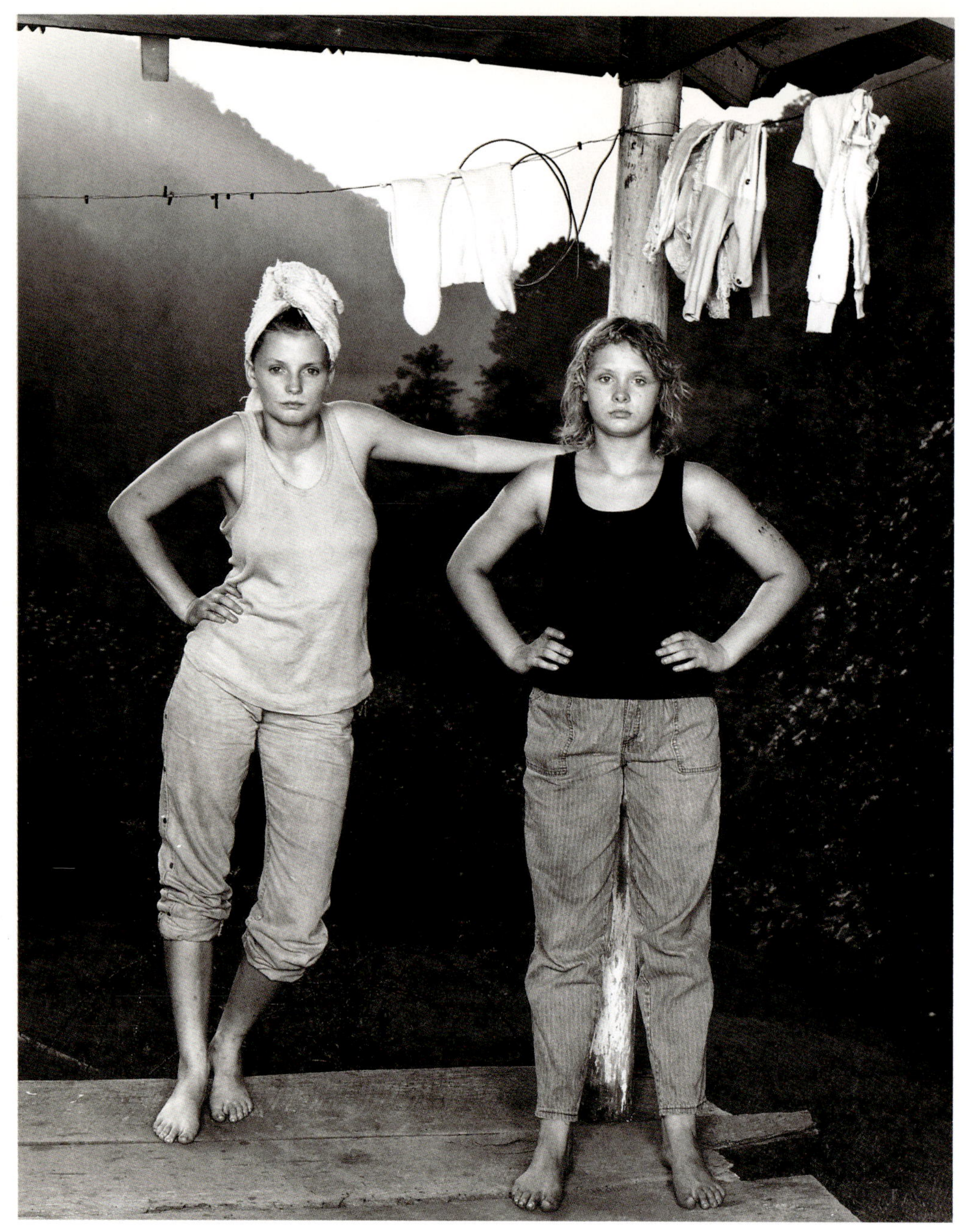

APPALACHIAN PORTRAITS

PHOTOGRAPHS BY

Shelby Lee Adams

NARRATIVE BY LEE SMITH

UNIVERSITY PRESS OF MISSISSIPPI / JACKSON

AUTHOR AND ARTIST SERIES

TO ANNE S. LEAF

whose spirit, strength and love
have guided this work
now for over fifteen years

Manufactured in Korea

Designed by John A. Langston

96 95 94 93 4 3 2 1

Cataloging-in-Publication data appear on last page

Photographs on preceding pages

Scotty with Banjo and Tom, Barwick, 1992

The Jacobs Girls, Isom, 1987

Art requires a delicate adjustment of the outer and inner worlds in such a way that, without changing their natures, they can be seen through each other. To know oneself is to know one's region. It is also to know the world, and it is also, paradoxically, a form of exile from that world.

FLANNERY O'CONNOR

Mystery and Manners

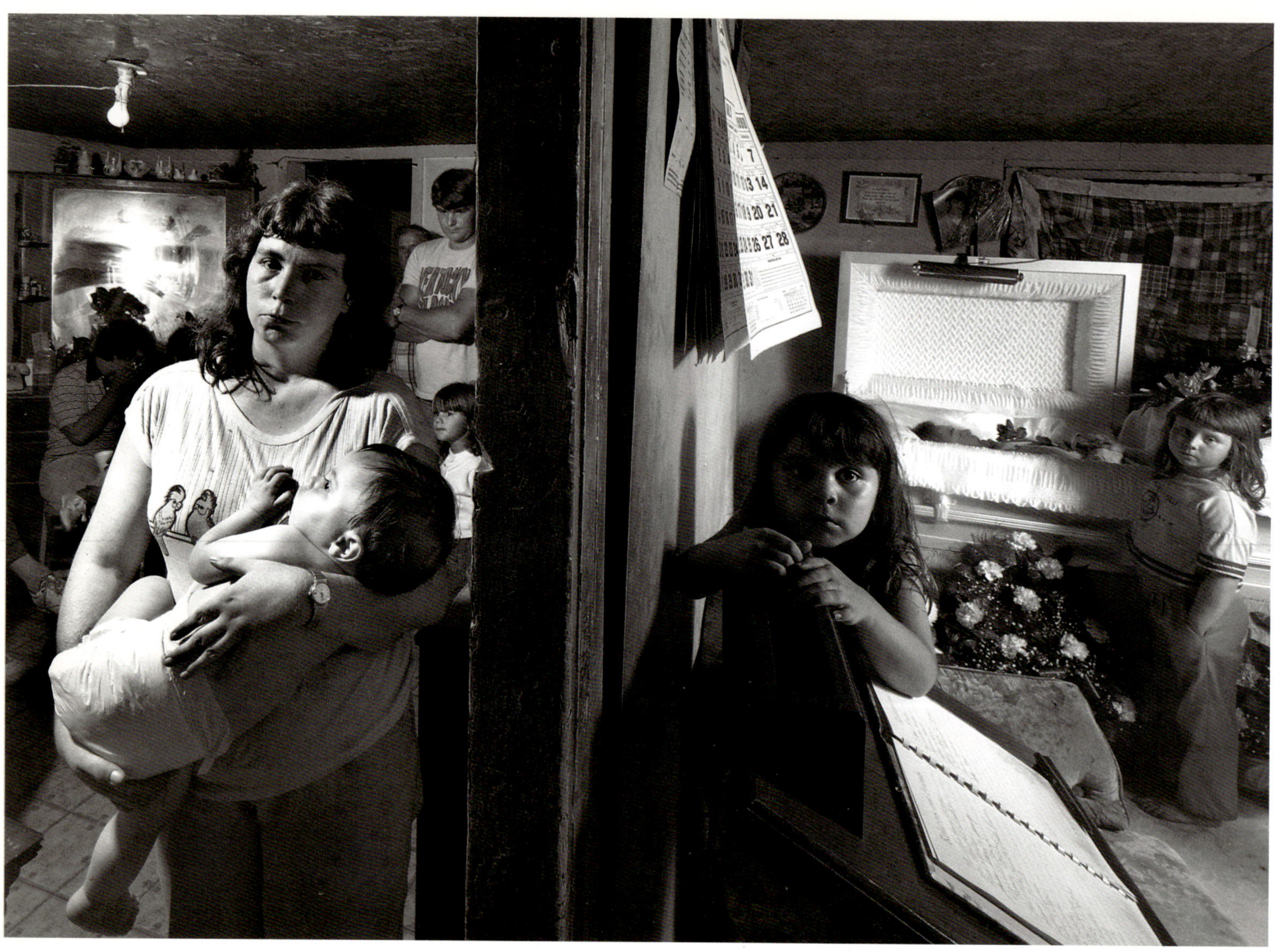

The Home Funeral, Leatherwood, 1990

PREFACE

These photographs, made in the Appalachian Mountains of eastern Kentucky, are part of a series begun in the summer of 1974. Today in Appalachia there are superhighways, fast-food restaurants, strip mines, discount stores, mobile homes, and the usual plastic that decorates the rest of the country. My pictures are by no means typical of the area and should not be interpreted as a general representation of all Appalachian people or their culture today. Rather, this is a study of a people cut off from the mainstream, bypassed by much of the ephemeral development of modern America. The subjects of my photographs exist in isolated areas and experience what most Americans would consider impossible living conditions. Because I was born in the region and have relatives there, I know the back roads and paths to which most visitors are denied access.

During my childhood in eastern Kentucky, my favorite grandmother was slowly going blind. I learned to walk the farmland paths with my eyes shut, to experience what it is like to be blind. This blindness was a great injustice to my grandmother, whom I deeply loved, and it was an unexplainable and unacceptable tragedy to me as a child. She gave me my first watercolor kit, and when I visited her, she would ask me to paint what I had seen each day. I learned to observe closely the world around me. I wanted to develop my own visual sensibilities so acutely that I could see *for* her. I know now that, as my grandmother was becoming blind, I was learning to see.

In *The Autobiography of Mark Twain,* Twain says of Hannibal, Missouri, "The class lines were quite clearly drawn and the familiar social life of each class was restricted to that class. It was a democracy." Eastern Kentucky is such a democracy, but its class lines are less rigid. All my life I have crossed back and forth between those lines, yet hating this social reality. My family was one of the middle-class families of Appalachia: I could afford to go to college.

As a college age art student, I discovered photography and became acquainted with the Farm Security Administration and Depression era photography done in the South. My professors always talked about this work in the past tense, as if the problems examined in these photographs were solved long ago and had little social or political importance during the Vietnam War period of my college days. The work of Walker Evans, Marion Post Wolcott, Russell Lee, and others moved me in an intensely personal way and jogged childhood memories. Those memories of Kentucky and the FSA photographs stirred me to begin my own photographic search. I also studied the work of Diane Arbus, Ralph Eugene Meatyard, Duane Michaels, and Clarence John Laughlin and later was inspired by the work of Mary Ellen Mark, Bruce Davidson, Emmet Gowin, and Frederick Sommers.

During my summer vacations I took Depression era photography books home with me and shared them with my family in eastern Kentucky. My uncle, a country doctor, upon seeing the photographs, said, "These people still live around here; they haven't changed in fifty years. You need to come with me when I make house calls in the heads of these hollers." My uncle was and still is a kind of folk hero to the mountain people of eastern Kentucky, and he made the perfect introduction to them for me in the early 1970s. On his calls Doc Adams packed his doctor's bag with medical supplies and equipment and a .38 caliber Smith & Wesson. When people couldn't afford to pay, my uncle would barter his services, accepting a bag of potatoes, a mess of green beans, or a quart of moonshine as payment. I learned how to trade and barter, to joke, to eat wild game like raccoon, squirrel, possum and rabbit, shoot guns, and drink. Most importantly, I came to respect the mountain people and to enjoy their company.

Since that first visit nearly twenty years ago, I have photographed throughout twenty-two eastern Kentucky counties, and I am known to the mountain people as "the picture man." Photographing in Kentucky has been an experience of continual discovery for me—new people, new approaches to photography. I am still amazed by what I find. Every valley is a new community. Although places may appear very similar on the outside, each one is different within. I may find a Holiness church service filled with frenetic psychic energy or a family that is quiet and remote.

The mountain people I photograph are not simple country people. They have a complex cultural legacy that resists the modern media culture that surrounds and invades them. Their religious and cultural values are passed along from person to person and handed down from generation to generation. For them, belief in a personal god is essential, and the spiritual world of devils and angels is a part of daily life. The only way to achieve greatness, in their eyes, is through spiritual redemption here on earth, for which the reward is eternal salvation with God the Father and Jesus the Son in heaven. They see life on earth as a test and a burden to endure; what matters is where one goes after this life. For the mountain people, material things may be beneficial, but they are often burdensome; education is good for those who are so inclined, but books and possessions do not necessarily lead to the gates of heaven.

Each summer I return to Kentucky with two or three hundred 8" x 10" glossy photographs made the year before, which I give to my subjects. They, in turn, introduce me to neighbors and friends whom I photograph, and the following summer, I return with their photographs. I prefer to work with a single subject or a family over a period of time. On the first visit I show pictures I've made of other family members, and I may not even set up the camera. Other times, however, I discover the family eager to have their pictures made, and I occasionally even get a photograph I really like on the first visit. If the first attempt is not successful, I study the image over a period of time and get better results the second or third visit, even when the sessions are a full year apart. A successful image results from an intimate interaction between photographer and subject.

The process of making photographs is important to me. To produce the photograph "The Home Funeral," for example, I spent several hours at a wake in the home of the family of the deceased family member, whom I had known. I arrived about five o'clock in the afternoon to join others, family and friends, who paid long visits throughout the day and night, bringing food and flowers. Standing in the entryway, I was flooded with memories of going to wakes with my grandparents, and I saw immediately the photograph I wanted to make: a partition through the center of the house divided two separate areas, two separate events—the formal parlor with the corpse on the right and the informal visiting room on the left. I visited with family members and stayed on that night for a prayer service in the front yard. Then at the family's request, I photographed their relatives and friends around the coffin, as is customary in the area. I set up my 4 x 5 camera and a location light kit and made more than fifteen different compositions as well as Polaroid prints that I distributed among the group. When the family had all the photographs they wanted, I asked permission to set up my camera in the doorway and take a few pictures for myself. As you can see from the woman's watch in the photograph, it was almost midnight when I took the image I had envisioned earlier that afternoon.

Every summer, traveling through the mountains photographing, I am somehow able to renew and relive my childhood. I regain my southern, mountain accent and approach the people with openness, fascination, and respect; and they treat me with respect, too. My psychic antennae become sharpened and acute. I love these people. Perhaps that is it, plain and simple. I respond to the sensual beauty of a hardened face with many scars, the deeply etched lines and flickers of sweat containing bright spots of sunlight. The eyes of my subjects reveal a kindness and curiosity, and their acceptance of me is gratifying. For me, this is a rejuvenation of the spirit of times past, and I am better for the experience each time it happens. These portraits are, in a way, self-portraits that represent a long autobiographical exploration of creativity, imagination, vision, repulsion, and salvation. My greatest fear as a photographer is to look into the eyes of a subject and not see my own reflection.

My work has been an artist's search for a deeper understanding of my heritage and myself, using photography as a medium and the Appalachian people as collaborators with their own desires to communicate. I hope my photographs confront viewers, reminding them of their own vulnerability and humanity. I hope, too, that viewers will see in these photographs something of the abiding strength and resourcefulness and dignity of the mountain people.

Shelby Lee Adams

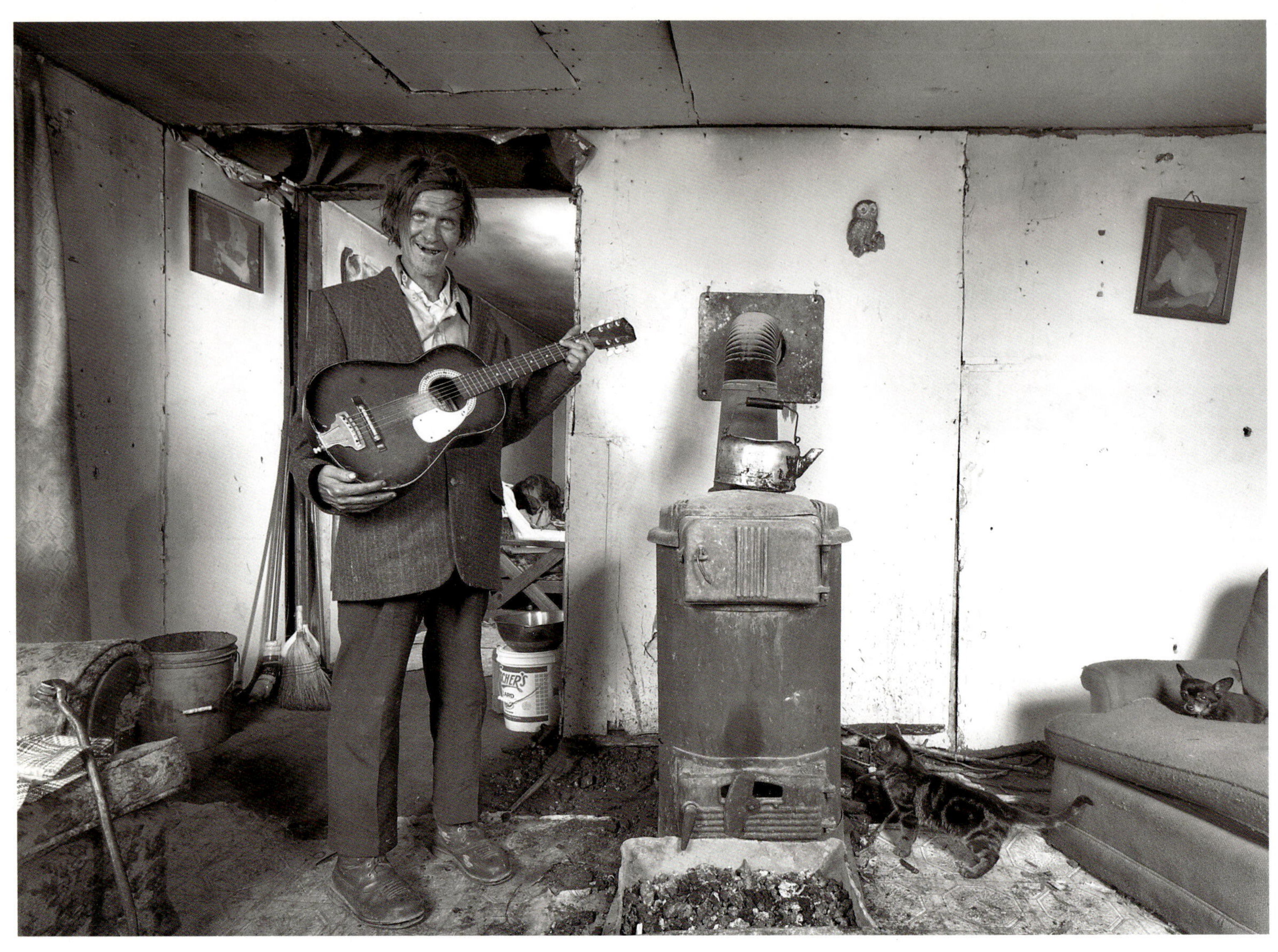

Bert with Guitar, Sloan Fork, 1992

MOUNTAIN VOICES

Lee Smith

These stories are based upon interviews that Shelby Lee Adams has conducted over the years in Kentucky and upon interviews and conversations I have had with people where I grew up in southwest Virginia. These stories are not "real," but they are as true as I can make them, as true as I know how to write. These are made-up characters with made-up names, who are not intended to represent the actual people in Shelby's photographs. But these stories might well be their stories—or, given a change in circumstance, these stories might be our own.

Imagine an interstate, then, any place in southern Appalachia—Kentucky, say, or east Tennessee or western North Carolina—then turn off that imaginary interstate onto a state road leading up into the mountains. Turn onto a smaller, winding road; then onto a smaller road yet, and keep on going when the pavement runs out, up the dusty rutted road with the little creek running down beside it. Then get out of your car and walk back up into the holler, up past the abandoned tipple, the rusted truck, back in time it seems, until you reach that trailer or that little house. People live here. Some people are still yet here.

Listen. . . .

FIDDLING BOY

Willie Bright was born on Christmas Day 1942 into a world gone wild with snow, the ridge across from the cabin all shiny and beautiful, to a good woman named Nettie Bright too old to bear children she'd thought, a woman beyond all that. Willie was plucked out of her womb and slapped and washed off by his grown sister Garnet and then set back on his mama's bosom for all to admire, and in fact he was a fine baby, fairheaded as an angel and light-complected and well made. *Thank you Jesus,* Nettie Bright said. She counted his fingers and toes. She smiled at her daughter Garnet who gritted her teeth and started in cleaning up the mess without a word. Solid yellow sunlight streamed in the window to lie like a blessing across the bloody borning quilt.

Nettie called for her other children, James, Alice, and Roy who was home on leave from the army. Their daddy had died in the mines, ten years before. *Now this here's my baby,* Nettie Bright said, *and I don't want to hear a word spoke about it. This un's the child of my heart,* she said, and that was all she ever said about the parentage of Willie who grew up bright as a new penny, his mama's pride and joy.

She got him a pony that he named Buddy and a little dog named Sue. She sent him to school as much as she could stand it, but never in bad weather, for it was a long walk out of the holler and down to where the bus came. Willie did not do well in school anyway, never able to focus his attention, the teacher said. He seemed to be listening to something else, something the others could not hear. At lunchtime he sat by himself, eating the pork biscuit his mama had wrapped in brown paper. Sometimes at recess he would join the others in a game of tag or capture the flag or kickball, but his heart was not in it. He was only waiting to go home.

In the summertime he and his mama did everything together, boy and old woman, working the garden, wading the creek for him to catch minners and crawdads, hitching a ride into town on a Saturday when she'd give him a dime for the picture show so he could see the cowboys and Indians. She'd wait across the street, on a bench in front of the courthouse, for him to come out of the show. This is where Willie Bright first heard old man Hull Jennings on the banjo and asked if he could hold it himself, please sir, and when old man Jennings handed it over, Willie Bright's fingers curved to it as if they were bound to do so, as if he was born to play music.

Nettie Bright stood in the June sunshine outside the gray stone courthouse and saw it happen right before her eyes. *I have lost him for sure,* she thought, but this was not really true, for though Willie Bright did take up the banjo and then the fiddle and was soon known all over the county for it—they called him the fiddling boy—he still came home to his mother no matter how late it was when they dropped him off at the mouth of the holler, or how late it was when he got in.

But one night in his seventeenth year when they'd been over at a dance in Letcher County, and it was snowing and the bridge was slick, old man Jennings drove his Pontiac right down into the icy black river below. Old man Jennings came out of it all right. But he would never get over it, because his own son was drowned in the river that night, and Willie Bright lay in bed for months thereafter, first with pneumonia and then with some kind of fever that burned out part of his brain. So he would never get over it either.

Though Nettie was devastated at first, she grew strangely content as time passed and it became clear that Willie would be hers now, really hers to keep always, for all time, and this turned out to be true.

At first, all Willie wanted to do was sit in the sun and play his fiddle real slow. He also liked to make things out of little parts of other things. He would do this all day long. Then he got so he liked to walk down the road. He liked to walk up the mountain. Every time he walked somewhere, he brought something home—a piece of quartz, a box spring, a tire, a hubcap, a dishpan, an old radio somebody had thrown away. He kept these things in the yard. He walked farther and farther, he brought more and more things back home. They filled up the yard, the porch, the front room. Eventually Willie Bright began making musical instruments out of some of these things, and sometimes he'd play on them for hours, ten or twelve hours at a stretch. Though this music sounded strange and discordant to anyone else who heard it, it sounded like a heavenly chorus to Willie. As he played, his face was beatified. Old Nettie did not appear to mind the noise. She was glad of his company. Her heart dropped each time he left, and rose again each time she saw him coming back up the road carrying whatever it was. He'd wave at his mother and grin like the sweet boy he'd been. *Looky here,* he'd say, and show it to her. *Thank you Jesus,* she would say.

When his mama died, Willie did not seem to notice as much as you'd think. In fact he didn't tell anybody about it at all, and consequently she had been dead for several days when Garnet found her, coming by to bring them some pickle relish. Willie helped Garnet's husband Jethro dig a hole in the family graveyard up on the mountain behind the house. Then he helped them lower the pine box down in it. *She is with God now,* the preacher said. Jethro spit tobacco off to the side. Garnet and Alice clung together, crying in the wind. Their brother James, who had turned away in disgust on that morning of Willie's birth, had long since died in the Hitler war, and Roy had gone off someplace, as had Alice's husband. Garnet and Alice would take care of Willie from then on, letting him stay at the homeplace, bringing him coal, and Red Man tobacco, and vienna sausages which he loved.

As they all started back down the mountain from the burying ground, Alice's and Garnet's children ran and danced in the wind like so many butterflies. Willie was smiling at everybody. He leaned over to pick up a shiny black button with a red stone in the middle of it. He held it up to the light. *Looky here,* he said.

RAYMOND ESTEP

Now you can't never tell what a woman will do. She might turn sour on you, or get all eat up with religion, or take out agin you in some way. It is no predicting a woman. But a good dog will stick with you until the end. I have about got to where I favor a dog over a woman, that's the truth. I like a blue tick hound for hunting and a little old feist-dog for the yard. I had me one dog, old Shorty, that was the finest individual I have every knowed. Loyal as the day is long. And when he treed him a coon, he'd set in to singing as pretty as Emmylou Harris, that's the truth.

LUDIE ROYAL

I always knowed that if I obeyed the spirit of God, that God would let me take up serpents. So I really appreciate it. I give God the honor and praise for it, bless Jesus. It's a good feeling. It's a pleasure in the Lord. Through the anointing of God is the only time you can handle the serpent and not get bit. What you do is, you've got to get your mind plumb off of everything on earth and fix it on the Lord. You get your mind *directly* on the Lord. When He gets ready to come on you, He'll come, and when He gets ready to go, He leaves. Oh honey, it's too good to explain. When He comes on you, it's a feeling you can't explain.

Chill bumps comes over you, your arms and your hands gets numb. You hear that cold wind blow, and you get a kindly cold feeling that comes through your heart. Then you know that you can do these things, and they is no harm in it. When God comes on you, you can do anything through His anointing. Anything. You feel your hands drawing to do something. Now when the Lord leads you to do something, you've got to do it *then,* honey, right then while the Lord is leading you to do it and while He is giving you the power over it. While you are anointed in the spirit. You can't do it after while.

But while He is on you, you can reach right in there and pick up Old Mister Serpent and he will not bite you, honey, you have got power over him. Power in the Lord. He can soothe the serpent. He can squench the violence of fire. I have reached into the heating stove and got up the coals, they was red hot, and carried them plumb across the house and back, and after the service was over, they was some that come and wanted to see my hands and they was not burned, nor scorched, nor nothing. Nary a blister, honey. Nary a blister to show. And I have been blessed to drink poison, honey, many times. I have drunk strychnine. I have drunk Red Devil lye. My boy cried to see me do it but he knowed better than to try and stop me, for when the spirit comes on you you've got to let Him work. You've got to let Him have His way.

Junior? Well, he was a Holiness child, honey, just like me. I reckon my daddy was the one that handed me my first serpent, when I was not but about 5 or 6 years old. Handed me a copperhead, just like that. I took to it, even then. I took to it. But a serpent won't bite a child anyway honey, so there's no danger in it. Children are born into the innocence and holiness of the Lord. They can handle serpents just fine. Nothing happens to them under the age of 12.

Why then they become outcast of the church, and the only way to get back to the Lord is to join up. Well, some will join right back up like I did when I was 14 or 15, soon as I felt the call and Daddy would let me, but others will run from it, and talk against it. They'll run far and wide, honey. Take Junior there. He's been in the navy, he's been in prison, he's been on drugs. But I always knew he'd come back to it. And when a Holiness child turns to religion in the midst of life, at the age of 40 or 50, say, it's the only church he'll go to. This church will not die out, honey. It's too powerful. You have to come back to it. It's in your blood.

Of course you can die of it. Daddy did, for one. But a person can die of anything, anytime, in this world. This world is not our home, we're only passing through. We can be gone in the blink of an eye. Most of the time, we are not given to know it. But when you've had the serpent in your hand, you know it. And later when you get back home, you look all around and your garden looks so pretty in the sun, and the world is so sweet, honey. The world is sweet in the Lord.

OLD MAN COONEY HARNETT

I don't know how old I am, nor what day it is. I couldn't tell ye, and don't give a damn to. I do what I do by the signs, and ain't got no use fer the rest of it, people included. I do what I do, and I been doing it. I don't lean on nobody. My people has been living up here on this mountain since the year one. I don't never go to town lessen I have to. I don't need nothing they've got down there but tobacco and shot, and coffee. Coffee's nice. I had me a old woman oncet that could make a good cup of coffee but she died. I've got some grown-up and gone-away children someplace. I don't give a damn. Used to be, I marshalled the mountain over at Hard Rock, I'd arrest em and send em off to Lexington. I shot a man twicet. Hell, I didn't care. I'd as soon shoot most of em as look at em, sorry sons of bitches. Now I don't do nothing but dig a little ginseng, time to time. You can get a hundred dollars a pound fer it, still yet. Them asiatics is the ones that buys it, thinks it makes em horny. Maybe it does. They is about a million of them little yeller devils running around over there on the other side of the world right now, horny as hell. Jest think on that.

MRS. RATCHETT'S OPINION

Folks say they live as nasty as buzzards, which ain't so. They have been shot at and rocked. They had one house that got burned to the ground, over on Stillhouse Branch. It is awful what folks will do to one another, do in particular to them that is any way different. What I heard was, Shirley had those two boys by her brother and her old man, when she was nothing but a child. So them is little incest children. Then she up and married John Roy Watkins who is a fine man, God help him, and he took them all on, and gives them a roof over their heads to this day and treats them just as normal as can be, right along with the other children. I have heard tell that one boy is real sweet, but the other one will run from you and hide up under the house. They say he will put anything in his mouth. What I think is, I think it's nice to keep them at home like that, so they can be with their family and see people. I can't fault it. When Brother Bell preached against it from the pulpit on Sunday, I walked right out. I'm not going back neither. I'm going to find me another church to go to. Brother Bell is the one that told me my own little Donnie, that died, would not go to Heaven. It's not in the Book, Brother Bell said. I reckon Brother Bell thinks Hell is stacked up wall-to-wall with babies and cripples and poor little incest children that never had a chance in this world. What would Jesus think? This is what I ask myself. What would Jesus do? I believe I have acted accordingly.

JUNE BELLE BOYD AND THE PICTURE MAN

When the picture man came around here the first time I must of been 6, oh maybe 8 years old. I don't know. I was a little girl. Before he came up here, the only pictures we had of anybody was took at weddings and funerals, folks laying in their caskets. Anyway the picture man he'd come and visit with us a long time and take a picture of whatever we wanted him to, mamas and babies, children and dogs, and give them to us. He gave us those little peel-away pictures. Then he'd come back with real big ones you could put in a frame from the store if you got a mind to. See, here's Mama with all of us younguns, I wouldn't give you a hundred dollars for this one. I was the littlest, and Mama's favorite. She used to call me her possum baby.

Look how pretty Mama is. Look at her eyes. It is like she's looking for something out beyond all of usuns, out beyond the porch rail, out beyond the picture man taking the picture, out beyond the mountains theirselves. When I look at this picture I feel like she's looking for me, since I am all growed up now as she never knowed me in life. Because it was not long after that, that Mama had Loyd who was born early, and then she never quit bleeding from her private parts so that before we knowed it, she was gone. Mama never was very strong, and not as big as a minute. What I think is, she was just wore out. Taking care of Daddy after he got the black lung, and us to boot. Mama never would teach me how to cook. *June Belle,* she'd say, *iffen I learn you how to make cornbread, you'll make it ever day of your life. You'll never have nothing. You get your lessons,* she said. *I'll cook.* It's true, I was good in school. But then Mama went and died on us and I had to pitch in like the rest. My job was to take care of Loyd who was a handful.

I tried to go to school though like Mama said, whenever I could get there, until Billy Breeding come in here working on the new road, that is, and saw me at Johnson's store. *Where do you live at?* he asked right off, and I told him, and before you could say squat he was up here ever minute, just devilling the life out of me. I reckon he has turned my head for sure, he is the cutest thing. Here's a picture of us took in a booth at the fair, you can see for yourself how cute he is. Billy Breeding has got a slow curly grin and a way of running his finger up the inside of your arm. He's got on at the mine now. Daddy likes him.

So, I reckon we'll get married sometime, but to tell you the truth, I'd just as soon have this baby first and name it Boyd, after me. That's my name, June Belle Boyd. I'll call it Hamlet Boyd if it's a boy, this is a name I got from school, and Violet June Boyd if it's a girl. Violet was my mother's name. But I'm hoping that the picture man will come back before I have my baby. I want him to take a picture of me sitting in Mama's rocking chair on the porch, looking up at Hunter's Ridge. I've got it all thought out. *Just get me from the shoulders up,* I'll tell him. *I want a picture took of me all by myself. Just me.*

APPALACHIAN PORTRAITS

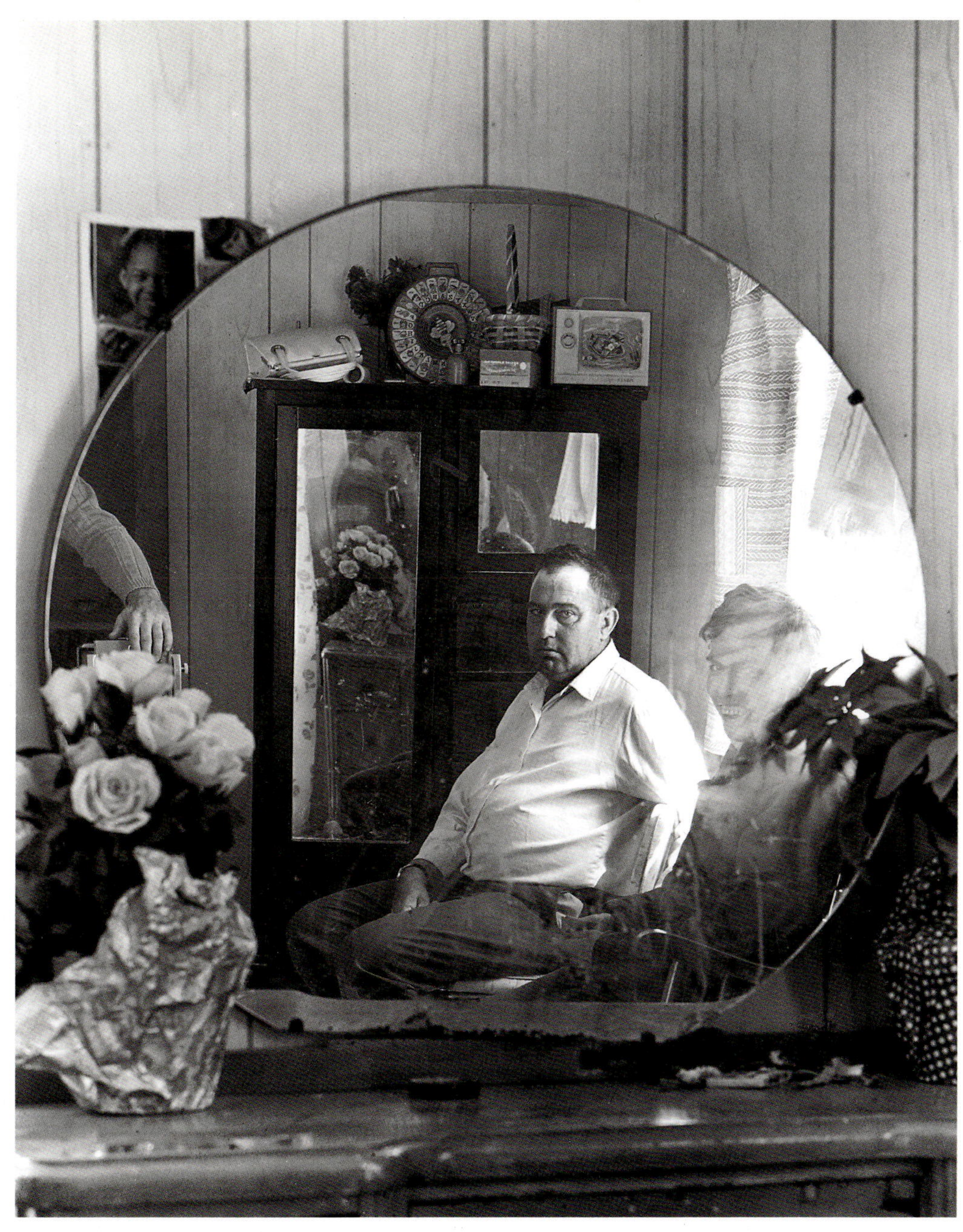

Christmas Day, Johnson's Fork, 1976

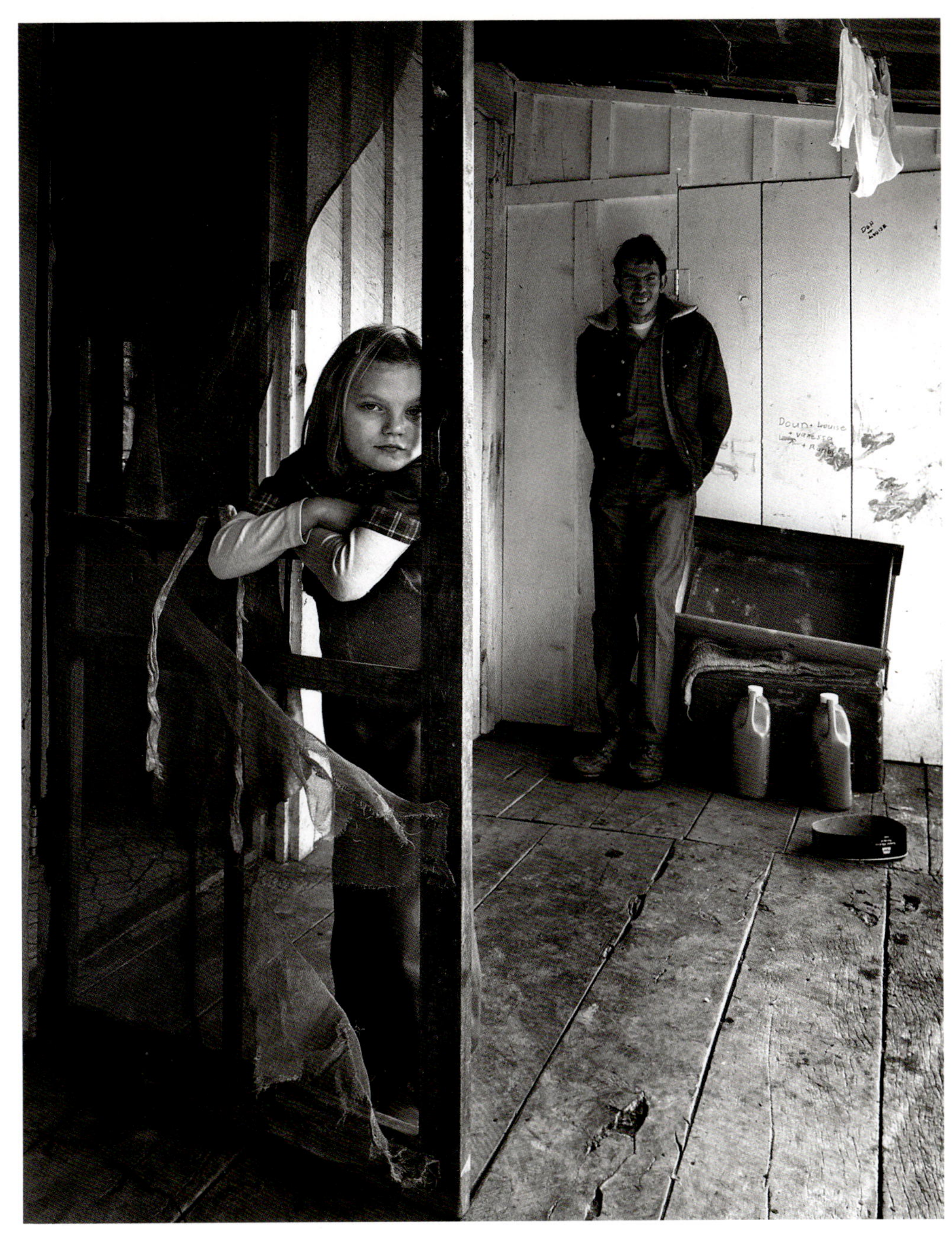

Melissa and Brice, Johnson's Fork, 1978

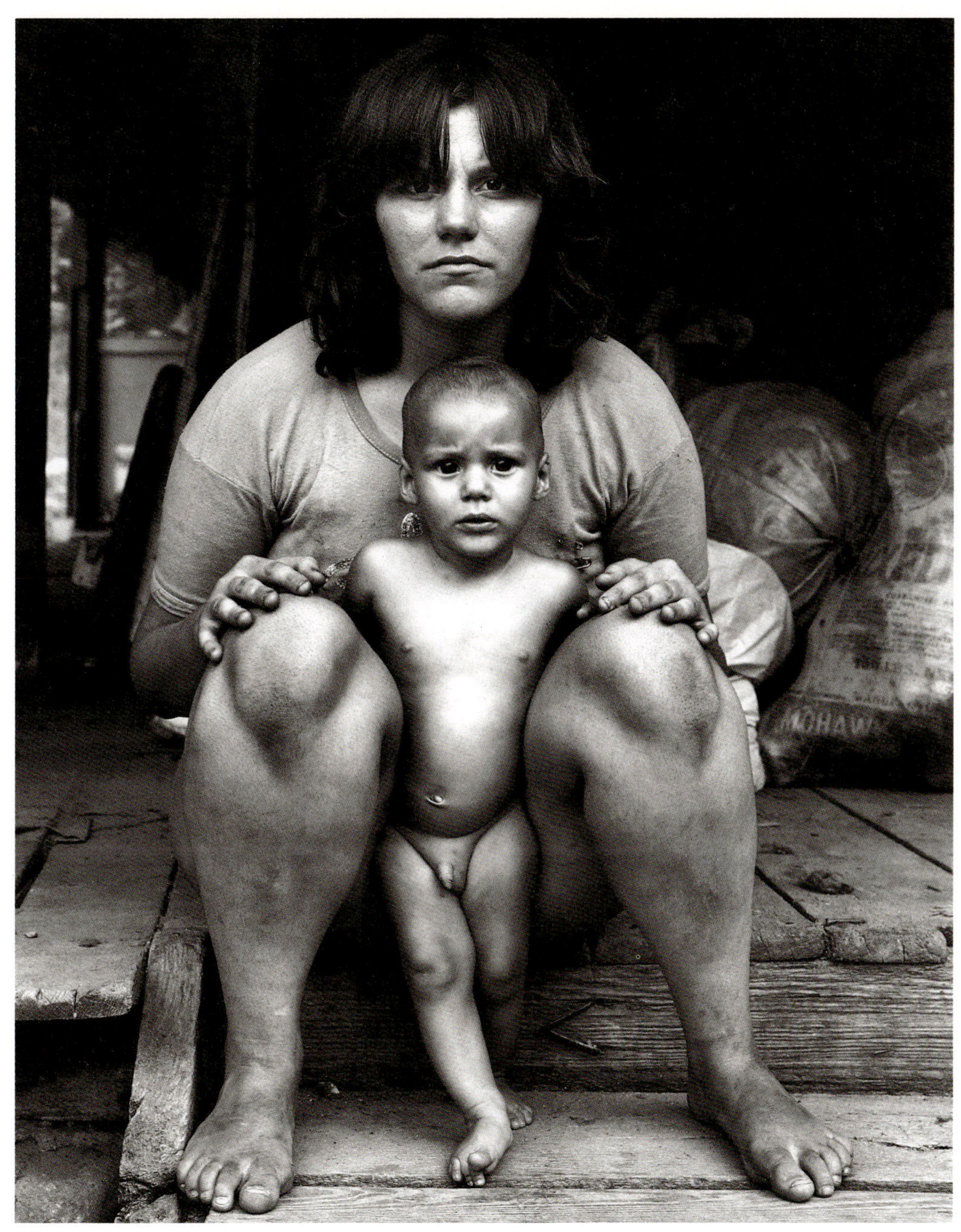

Correrine and Baby, Spring Branch, 1983

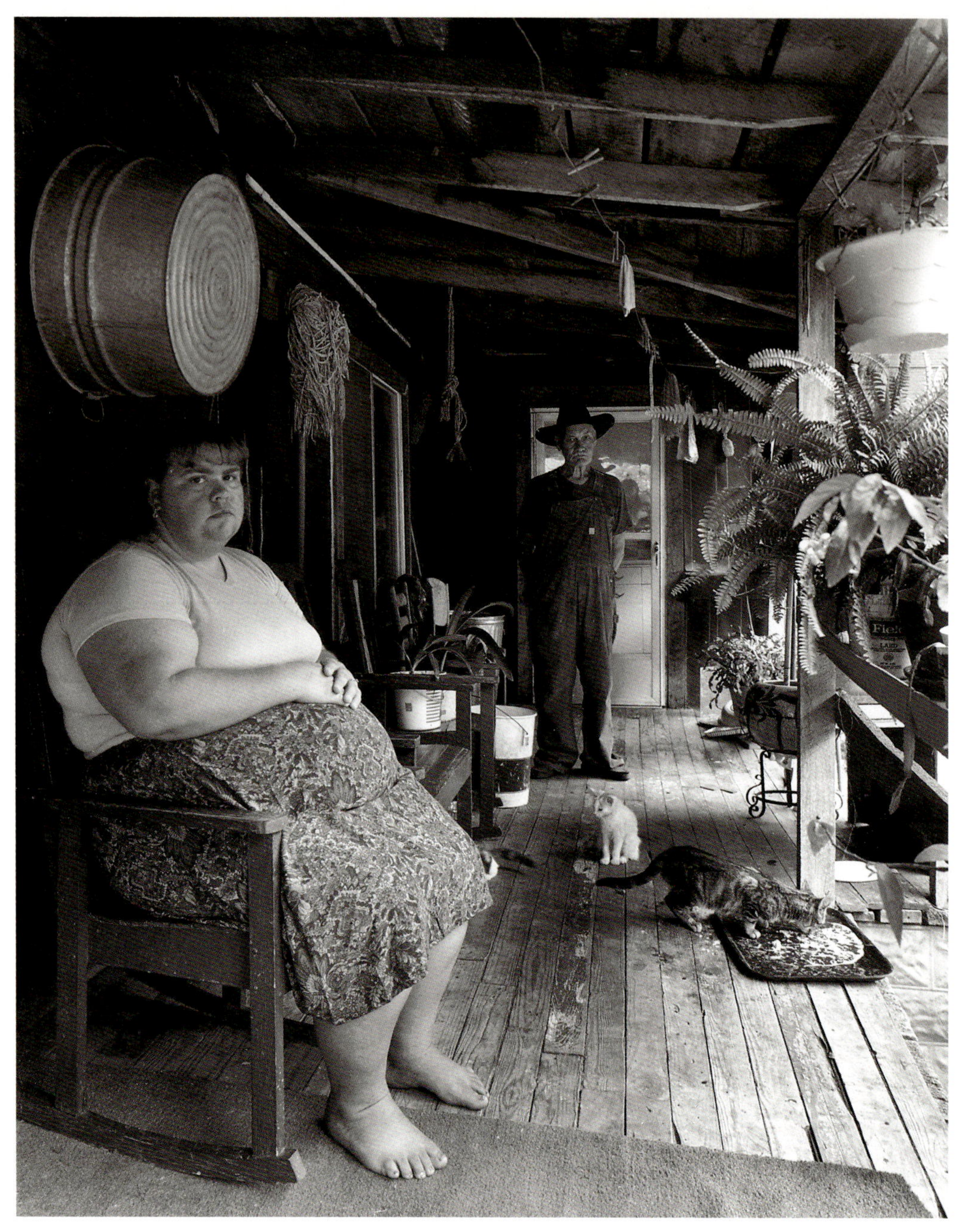

Mr. Wynn and Daisy, Camp Branch, 1983

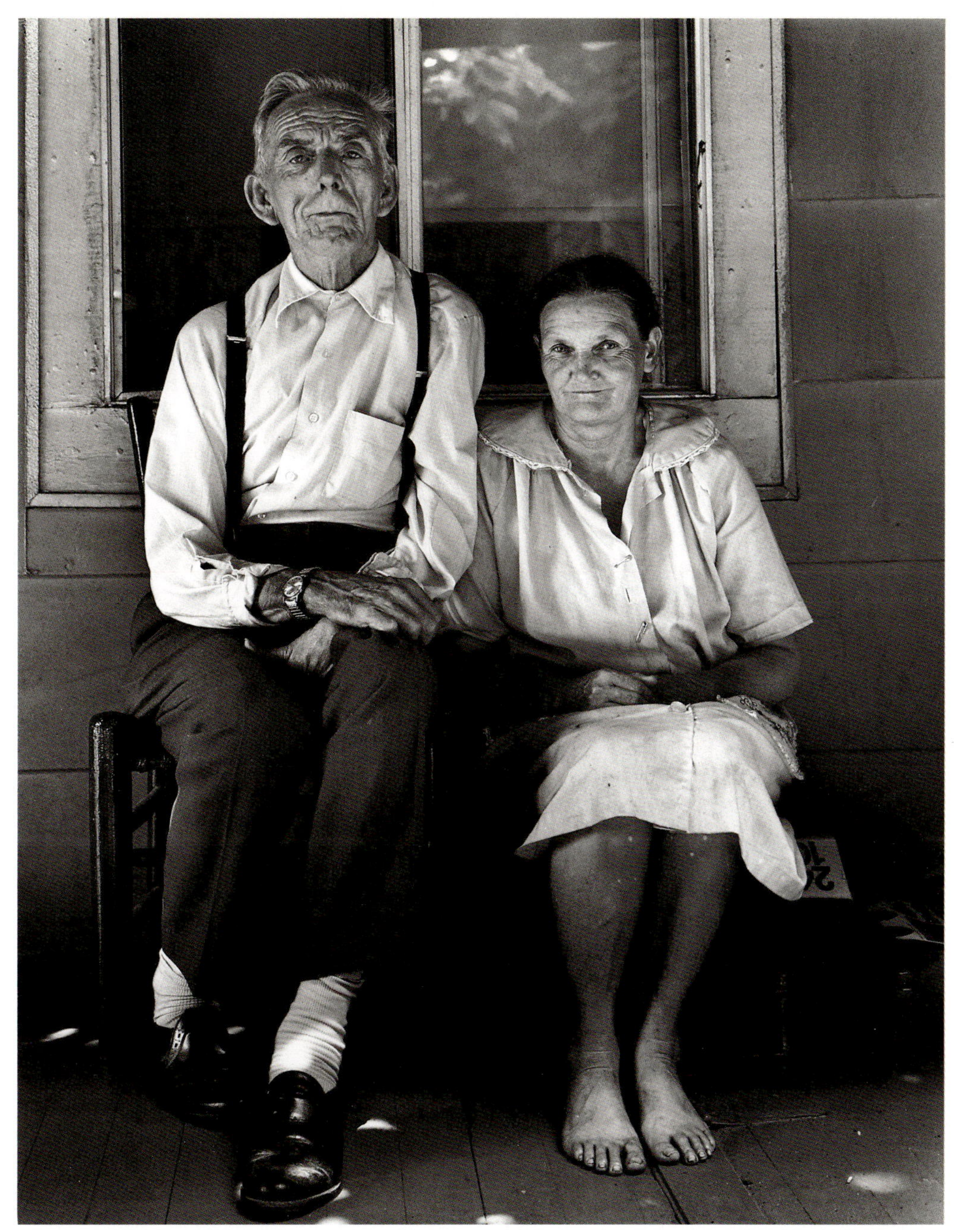

Kelly and Armeldia, Colly Gap, 1983

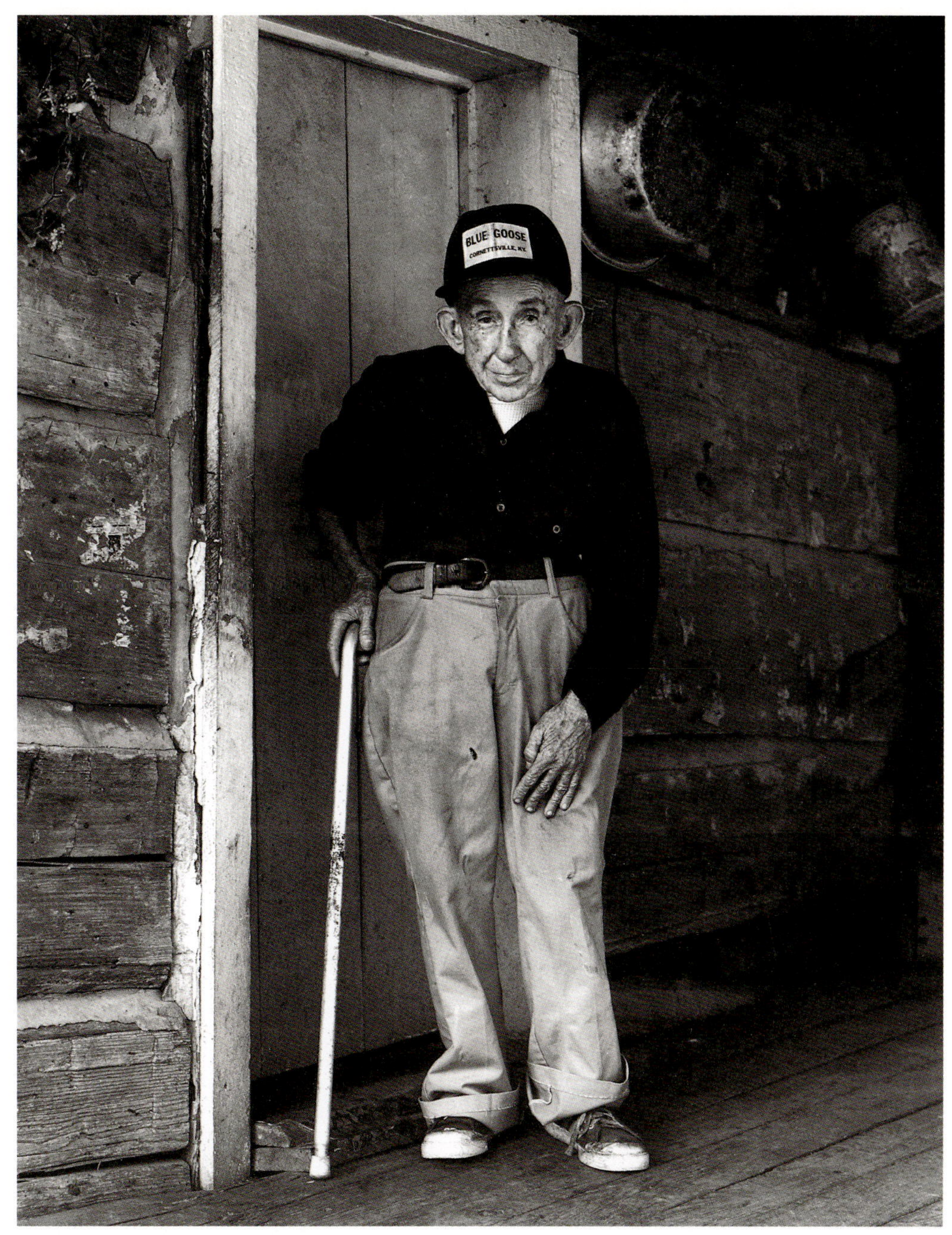

Mr. Dixon, Turkey Creek, 1985

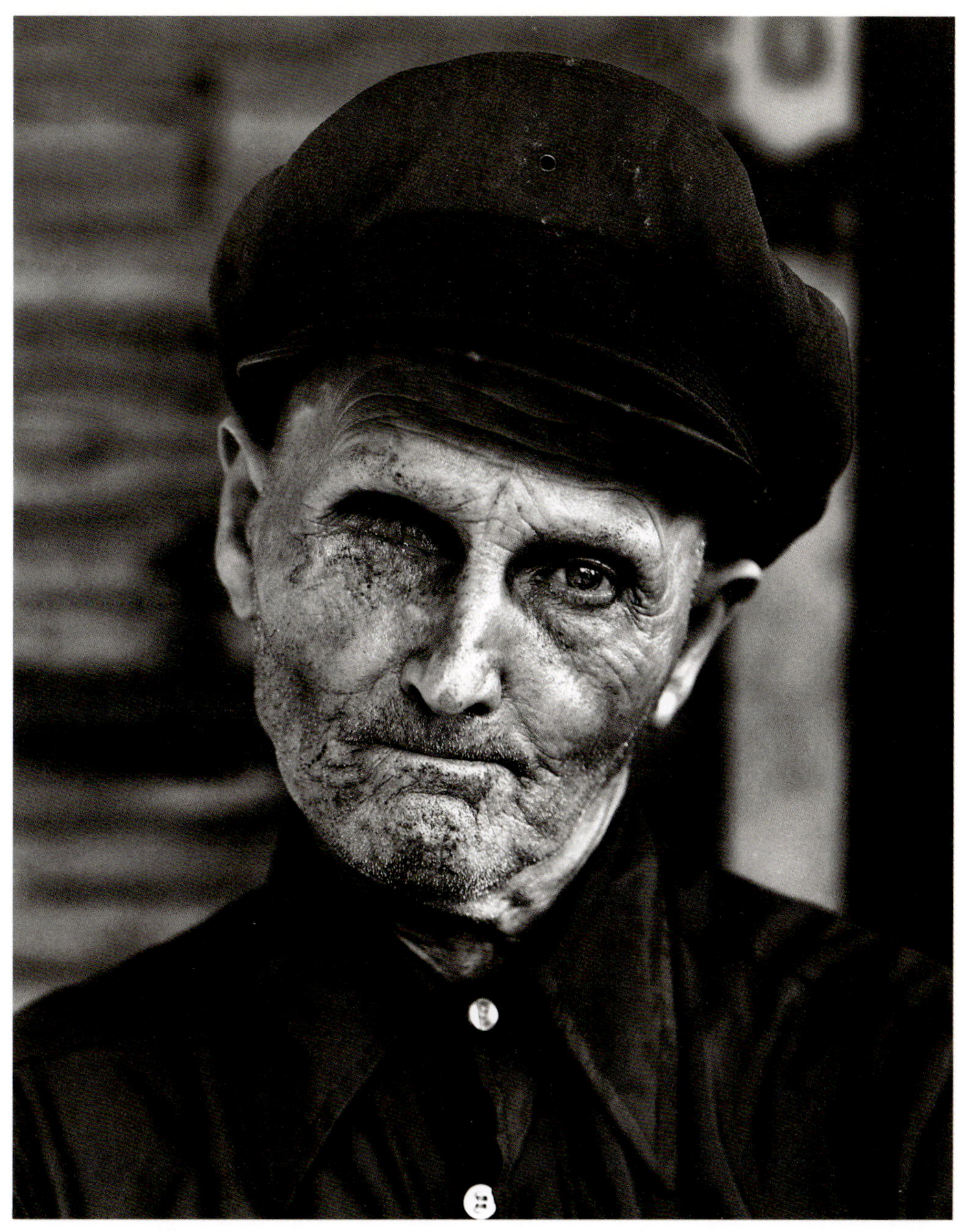

Lee Hall, Retired Coal Miner, Camp Branch, 1983

THE NAPIER FAMILY

BEEHIVE, KENTUCKY

Had sixteen children in my family—you wouldn't believe that, would you! Eight dead and eight livin'! Lord, they drank and get out and get killed, and everything. You know, you can't put sense on 'em. After they get grown, you can't do nothing' with 'em. But when they was small, they mind me good, till they got to be twenty-two or twenty-three. Now, Lord have mercy!

BERTHIE NAPIER

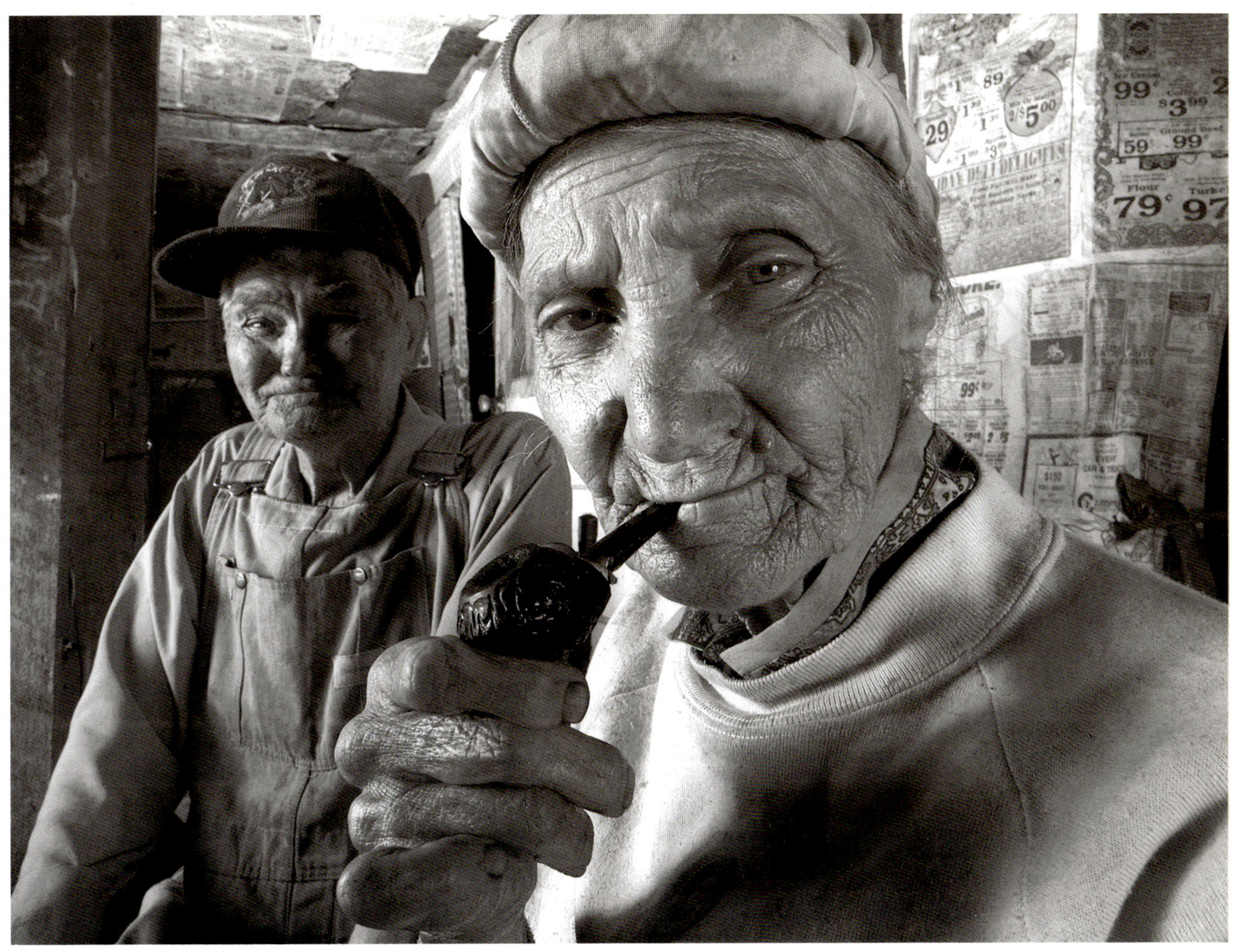

Berthie Napier with Pipe and John, 1992

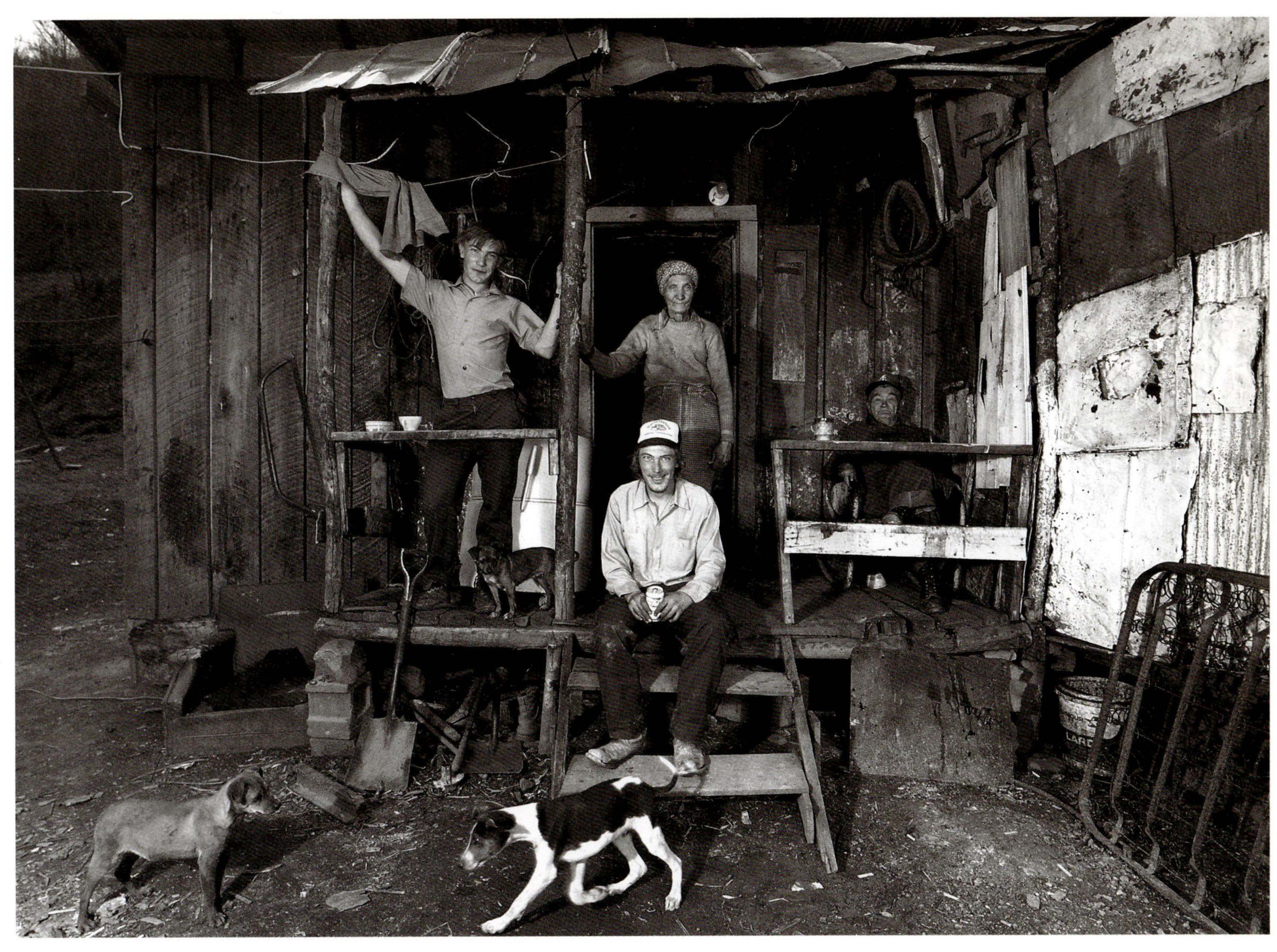

The Napiers with Dogs, 1988

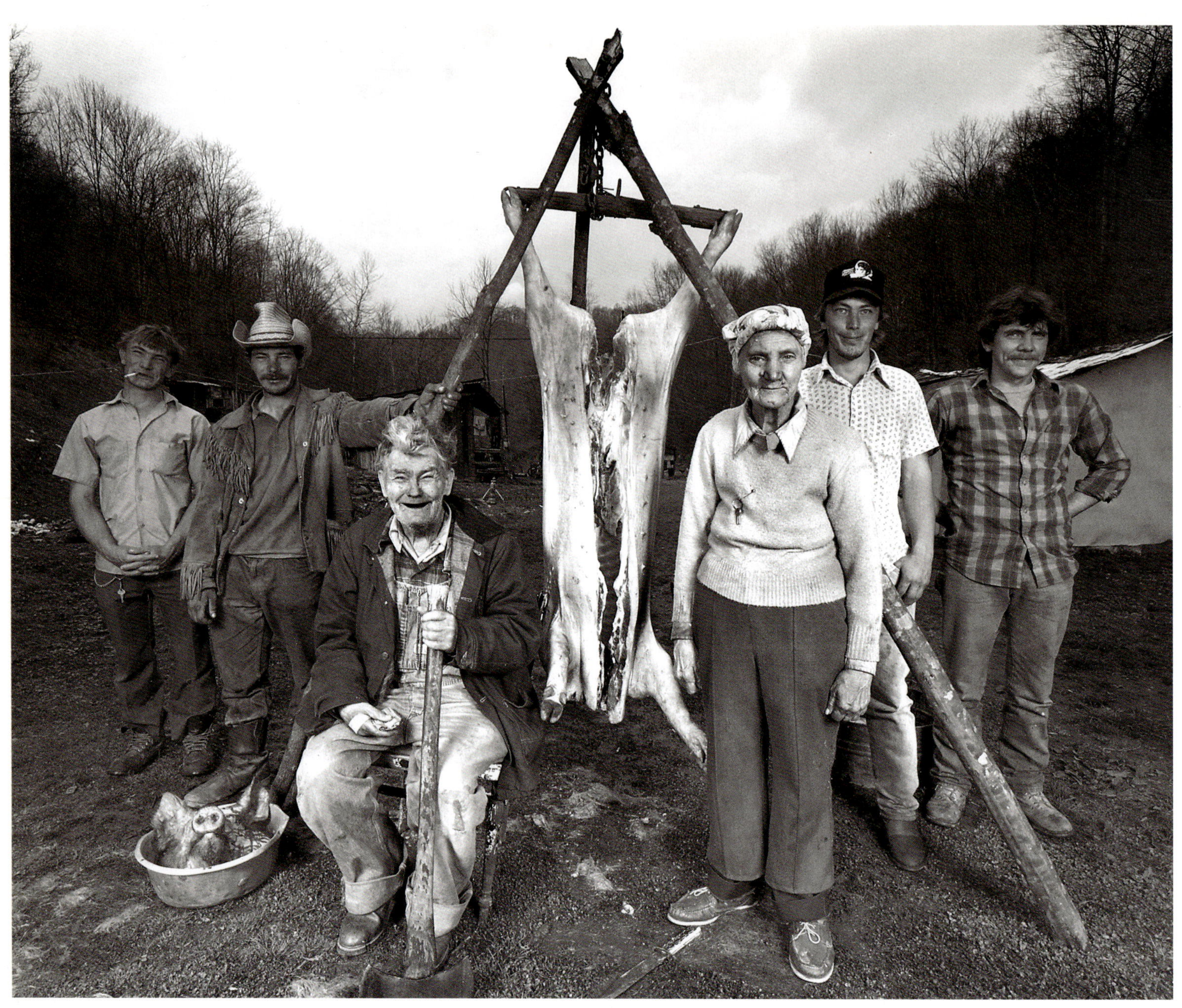

The Hog Killing, 1990

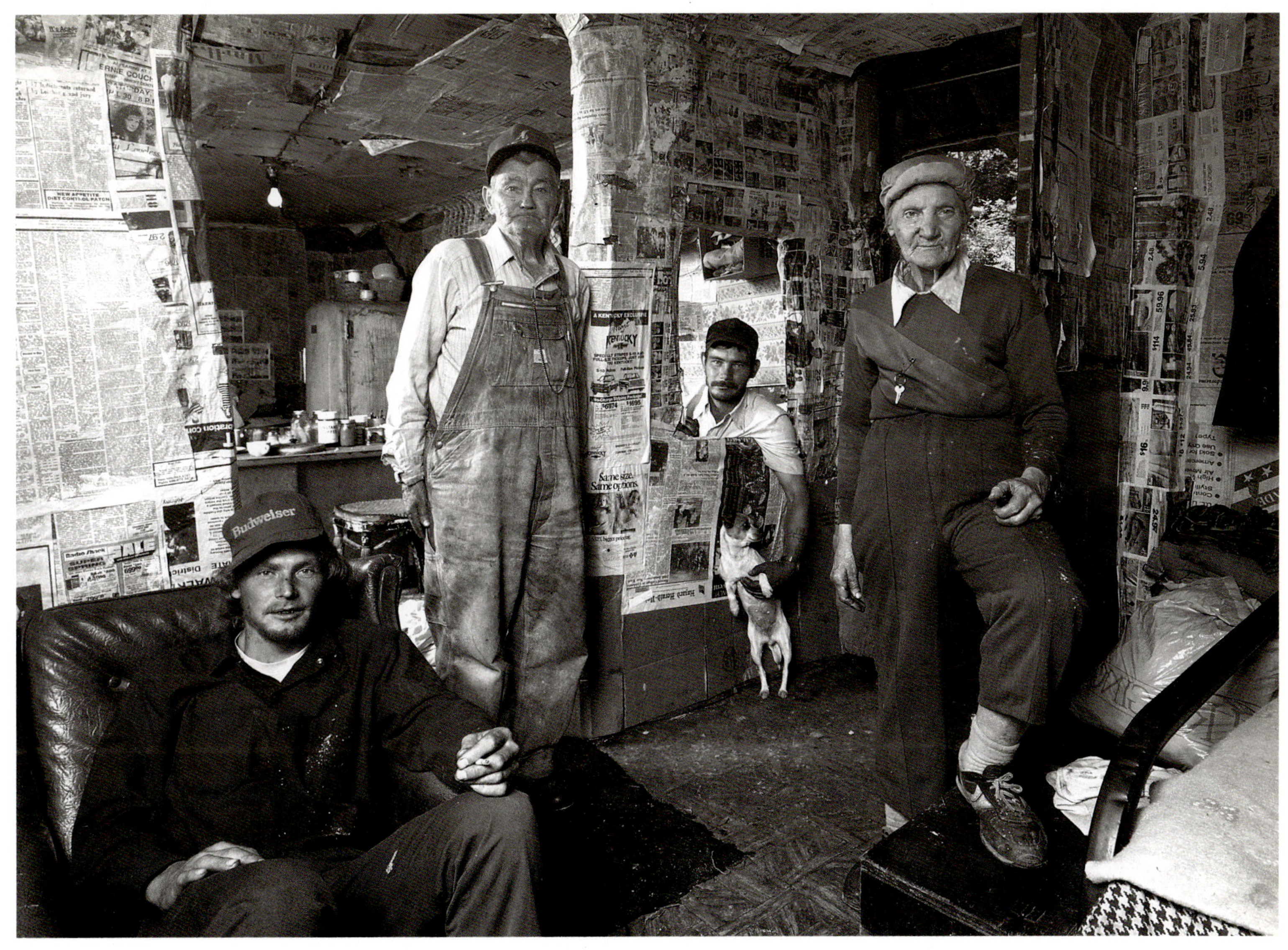

The Napiers' Living Room, 1989

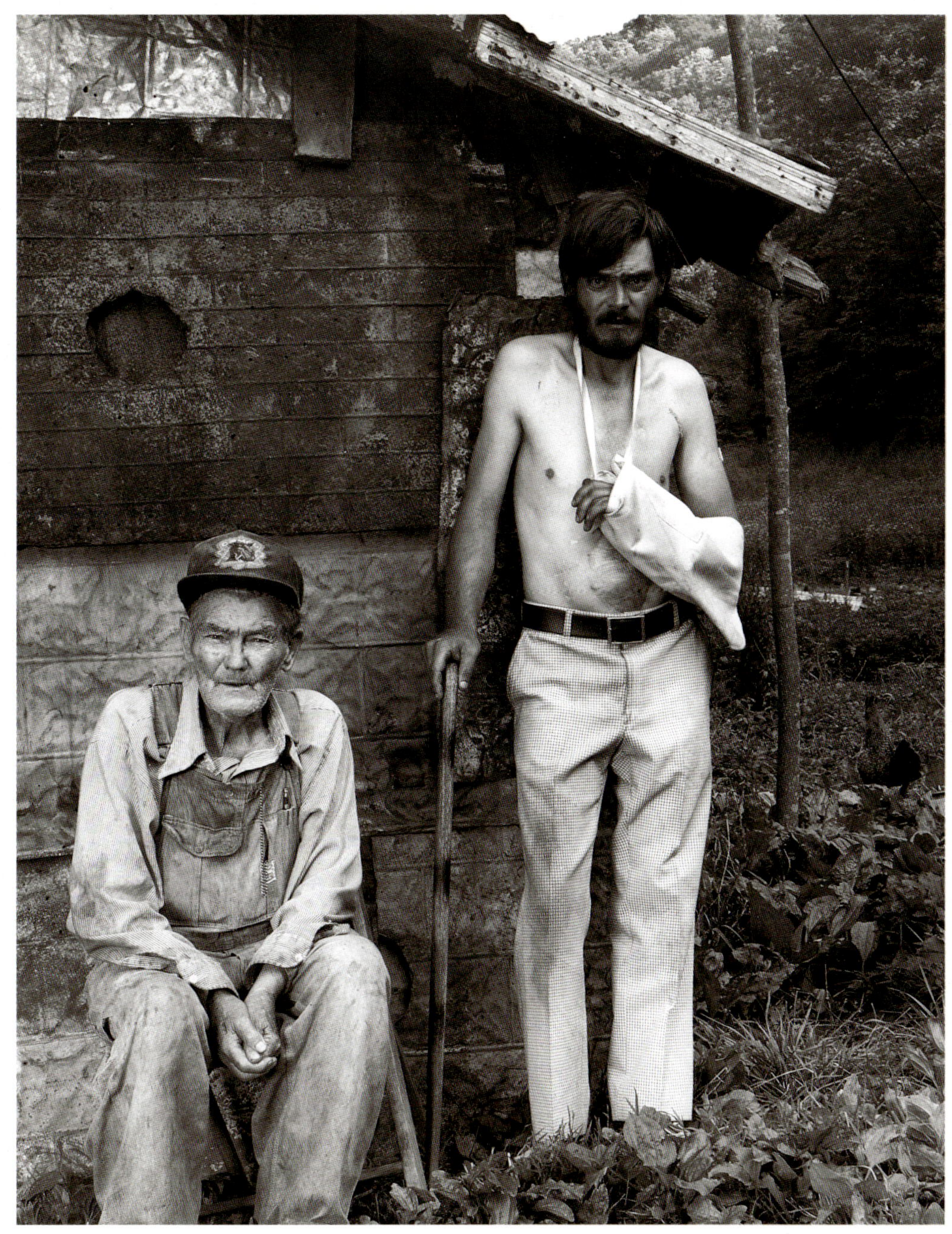

Arch Napier with Father after Receiving Fifth Gunshot Wound, 1991

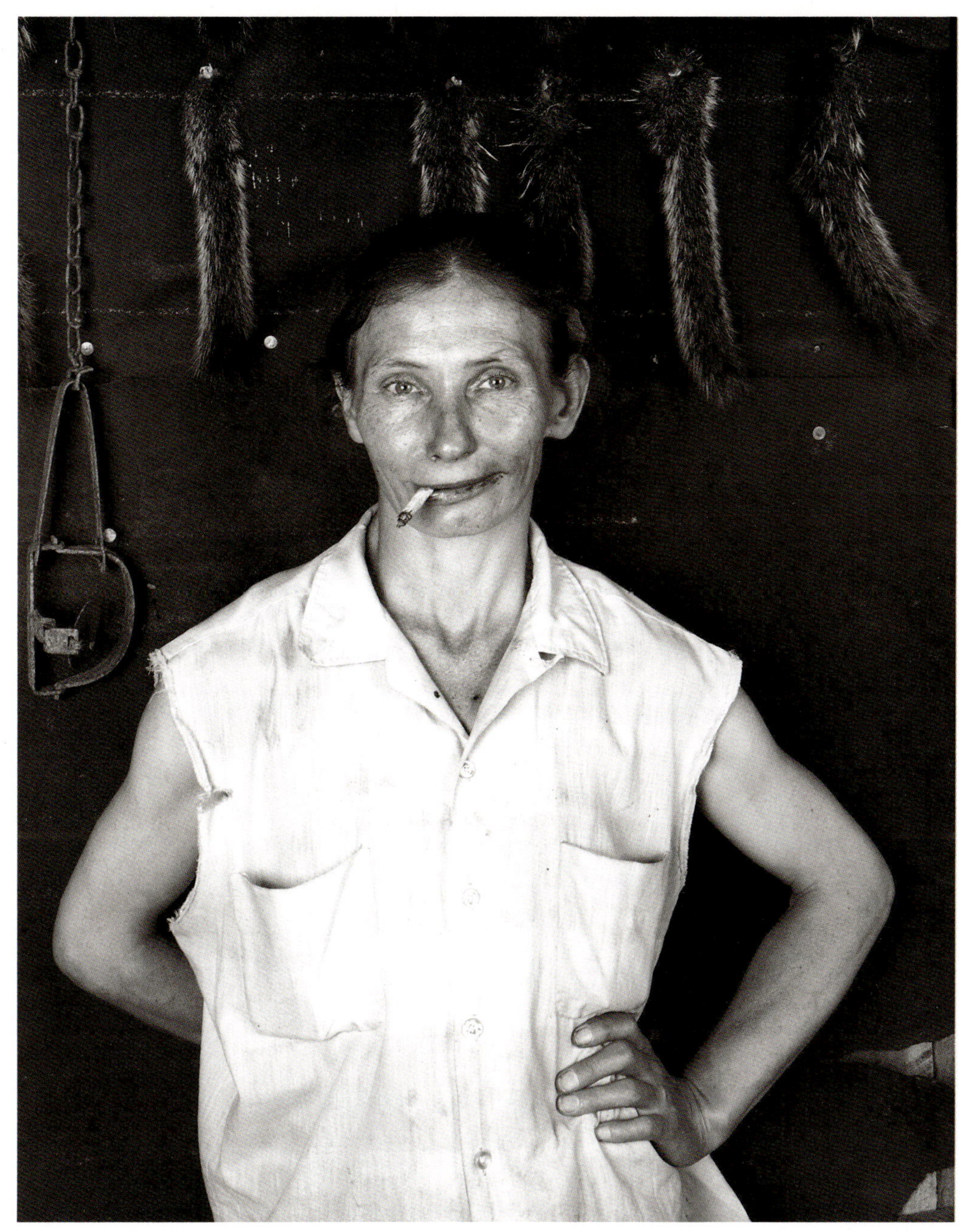

Mary Napier, Viper, 1989

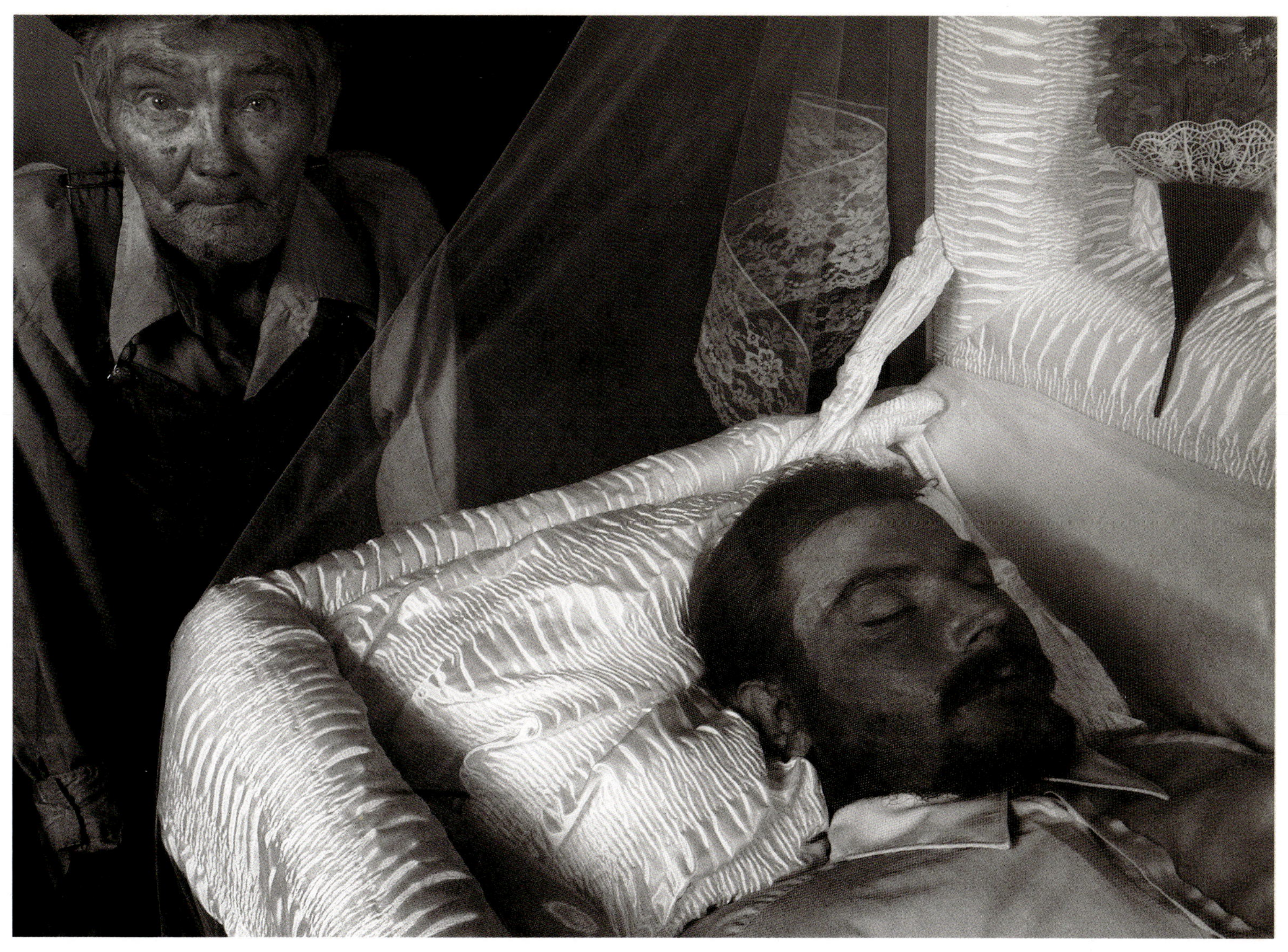

Dan Napier's Funeral, Viper, 1991

THE SLOAN FAMILY

SLOAN FORK, KENTUCKY

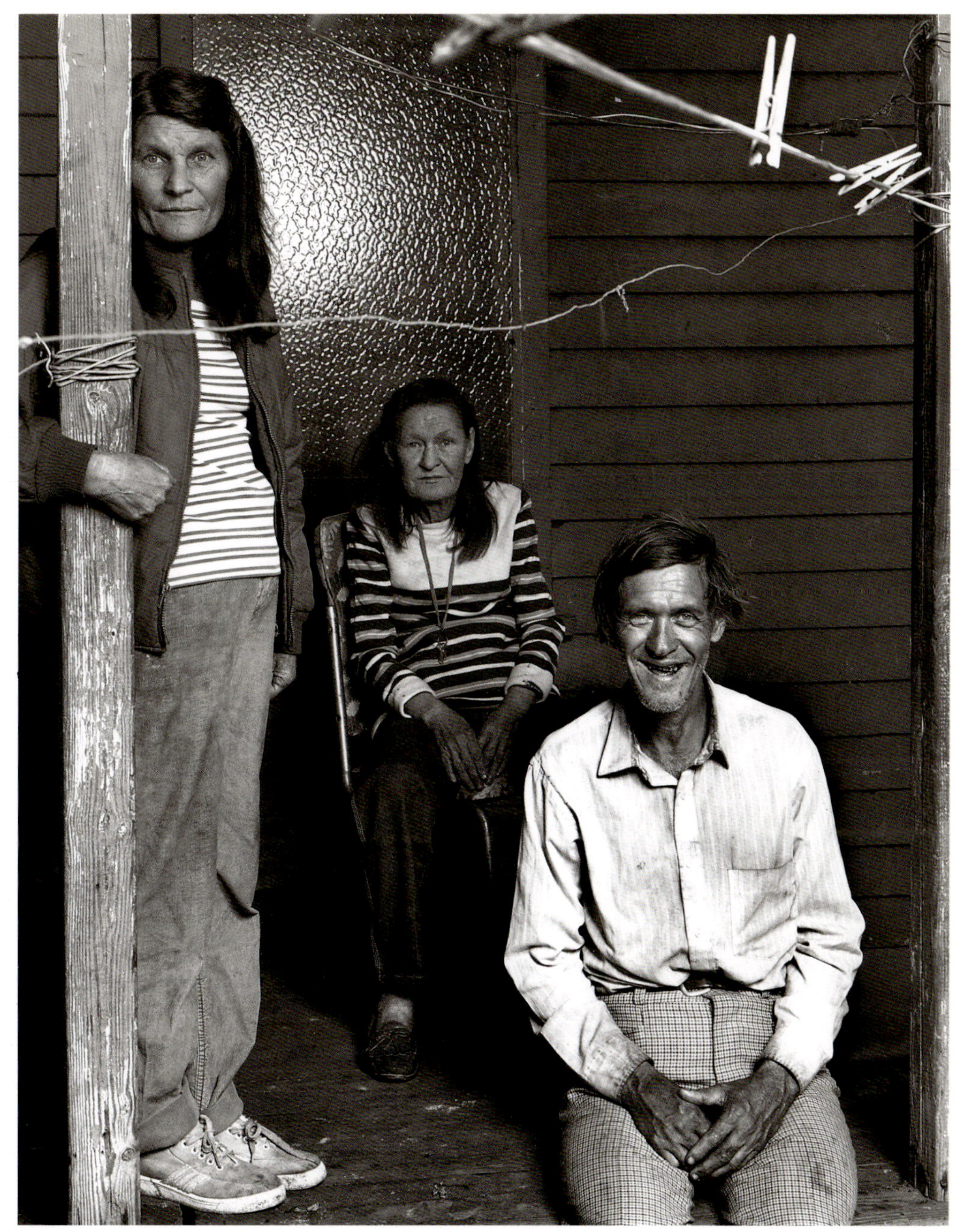

Sloans on Porch, 1988

BERT SLOAN, a local eccentric who lives on top of Sloan Mountain in Knott County, Kentucky, is the member of the Sloan clan on whom I have concentrated most of my photography and personal interest since I came to know the family in 1983. His family says that Bert suffered a sunstroke when he was in his mid-twenties and never regained his full mental and physical health. An aspiring musician until his illness, Bert carries with him several Jew's harps, which he made himself from rusty bed springs and Prince Albert tobacco cans. Sometimes he has as many as six different harps, each keyed to a different tune, and he plays them whenever the mood strikes. Bert has been nicknamed "the walker," because he often takes long walks on the country roads, walking until he passes out, twenty to thirty miles at a time. Sometimes the local police pick him up on the roadside and take him to the jail, where they give him a meal and call his relatives to come for him. He is cared for by his two loving sisters, Leddie and Lonnie Sloan.

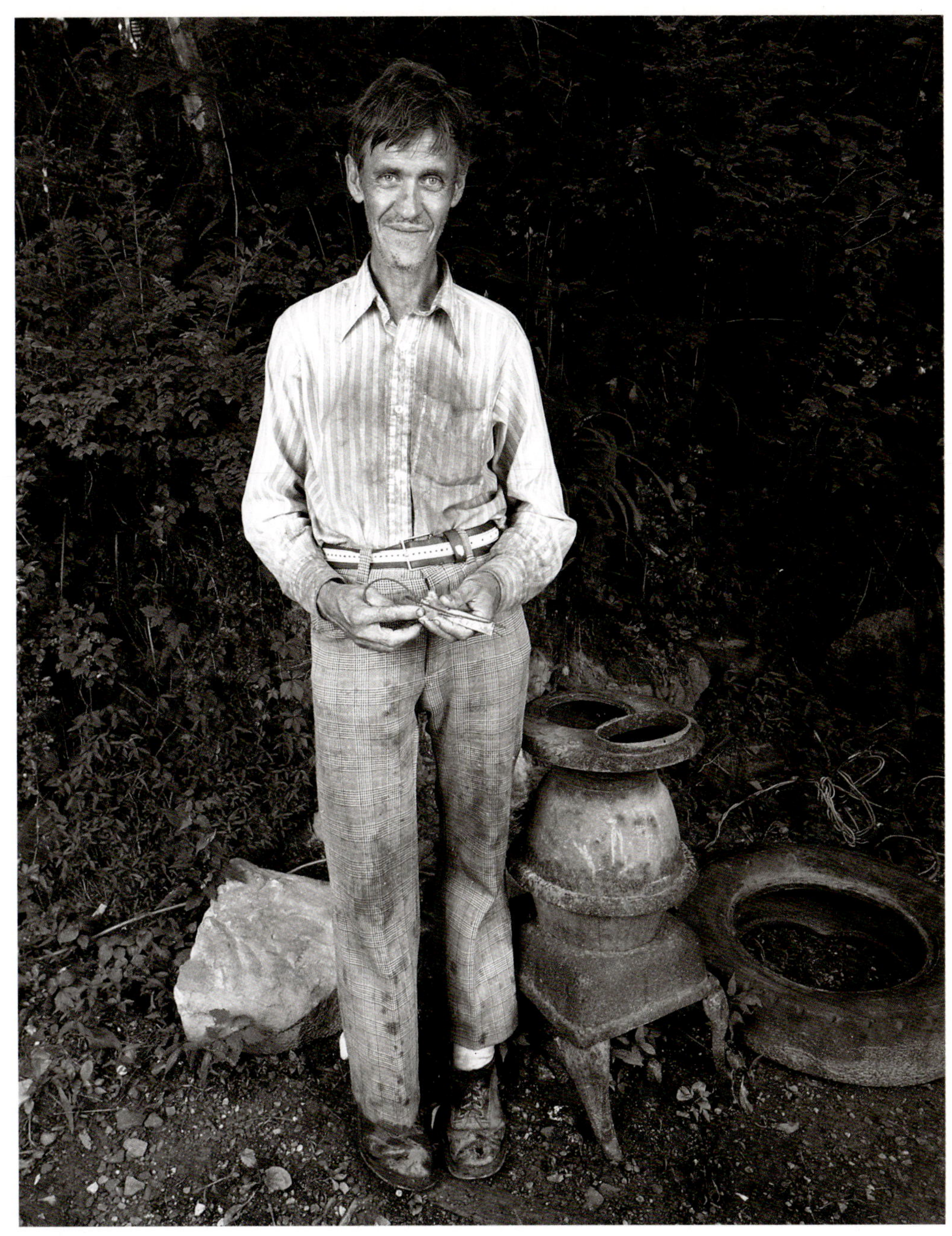

Bert Holding Homemade Jew's Harp, 1987

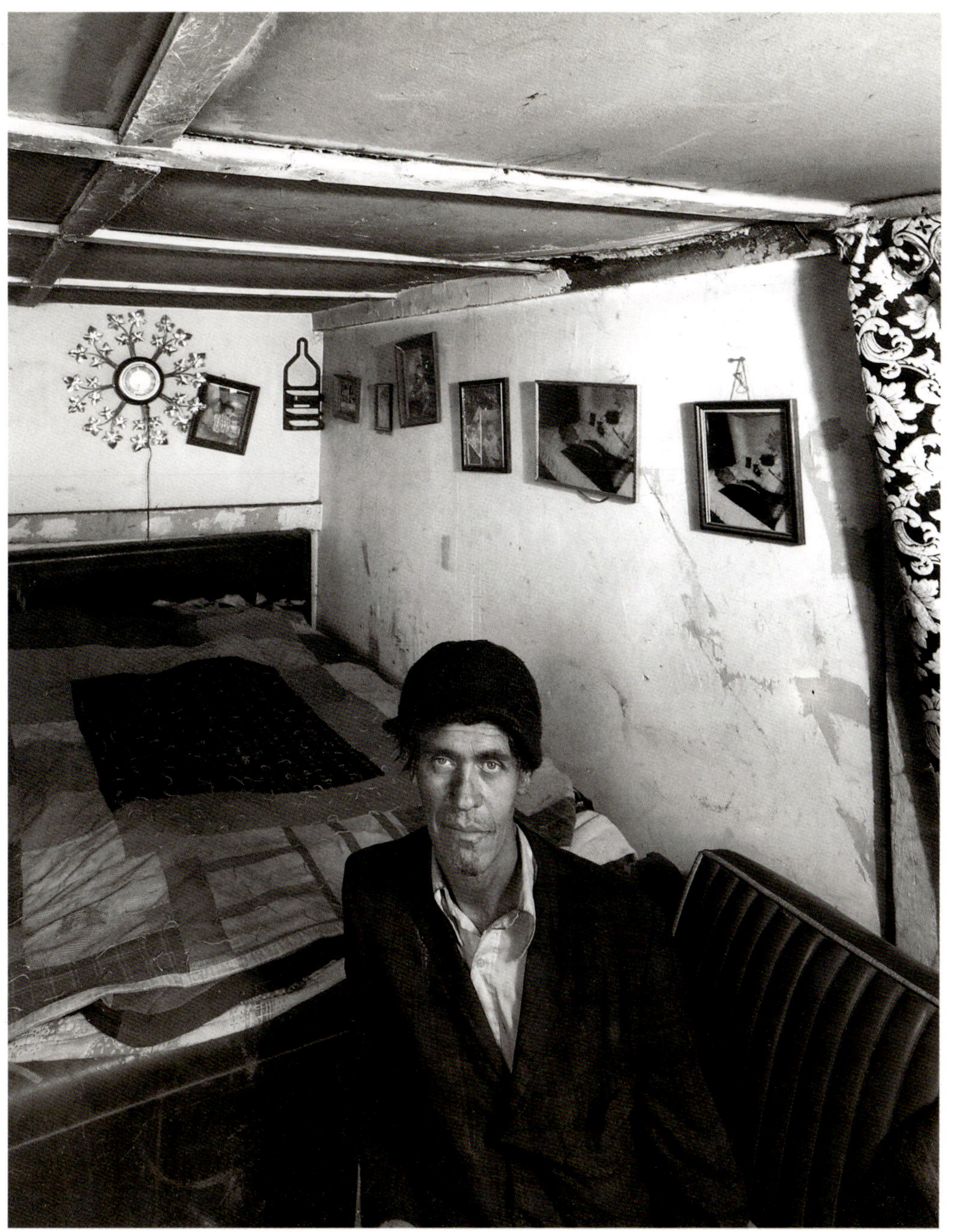

Bert Sitting in Front of Bed, 1988

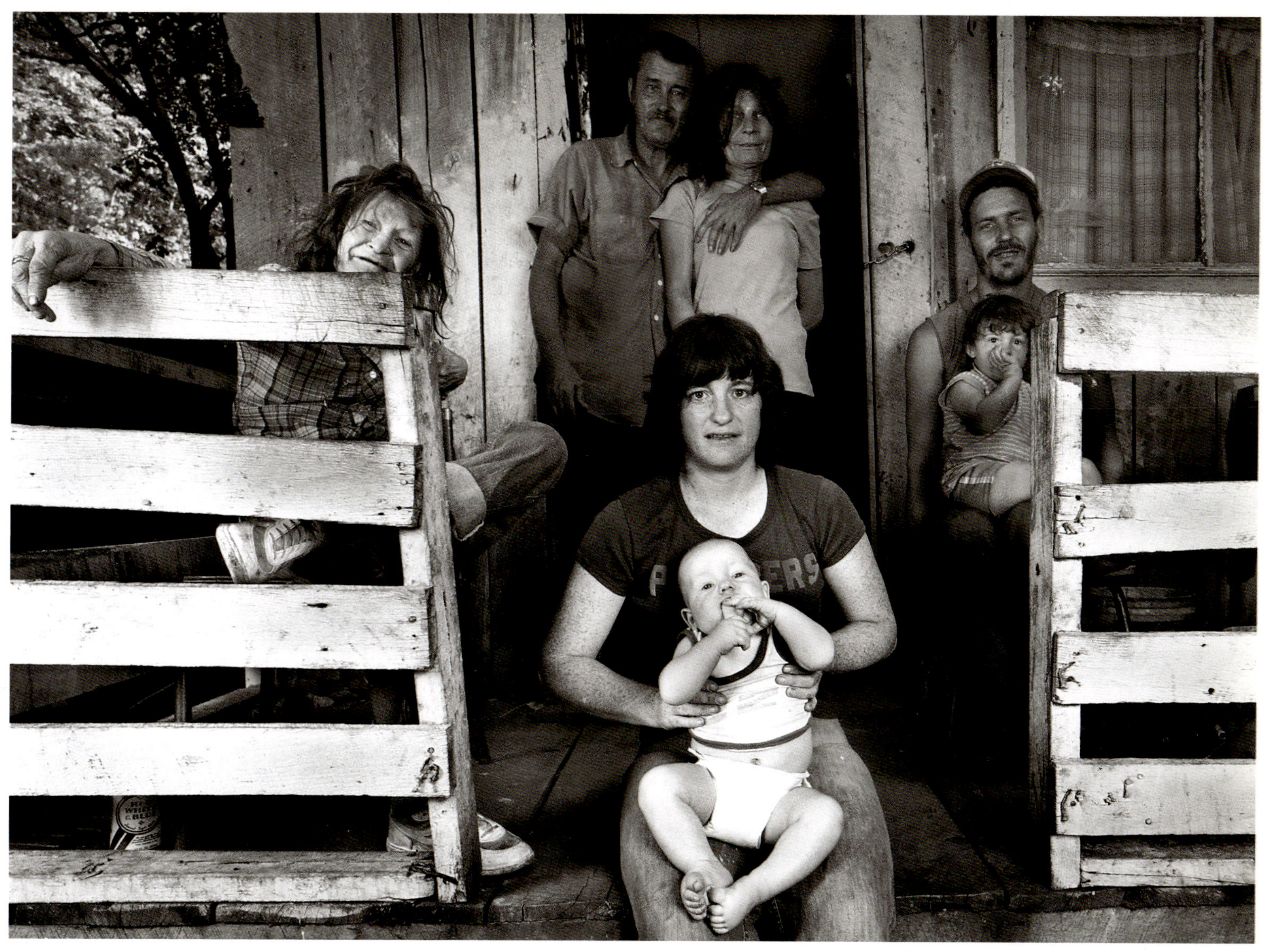

Fourth of July, 1986

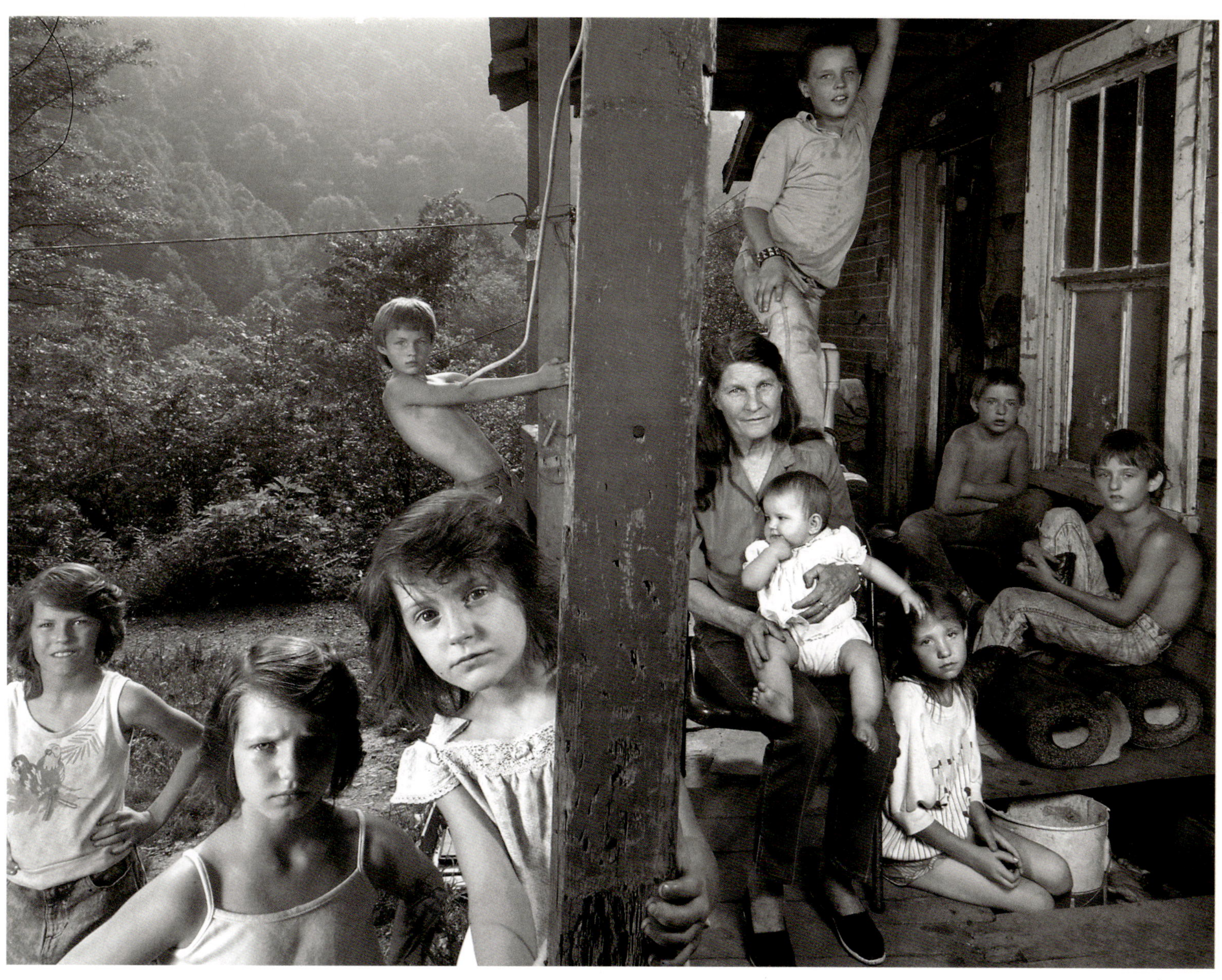

Leddie with Children, 1990

HOLINESS RELIGION

And these signs shall follow them that believe; in My name shall they cast out devils; they shall take up serpents; and if they drink any deadly thing, it shall not hurt them; they shall lay hands on the sick, and they shall recover.

MARK 16:17—18

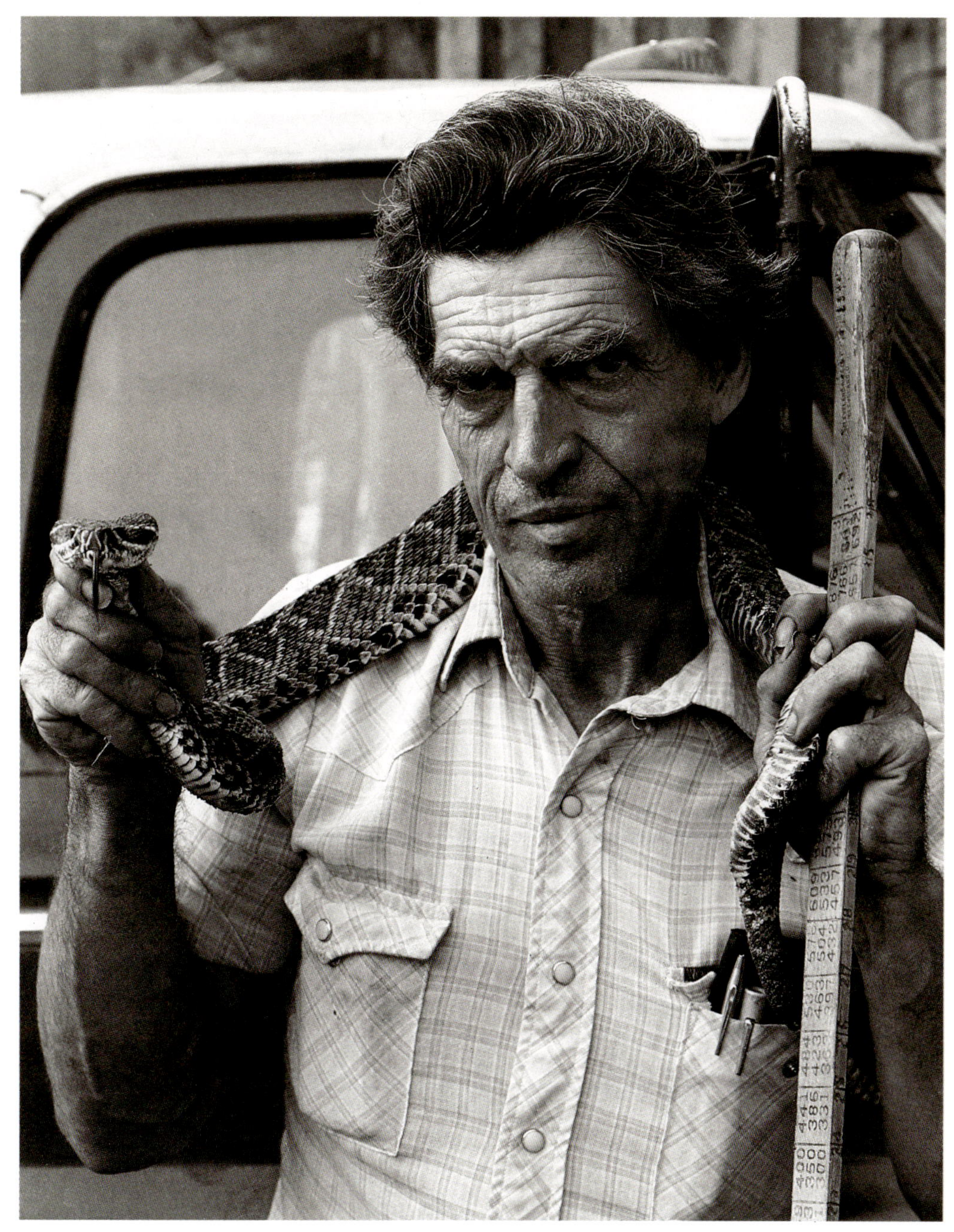

Snake Hunter, Red Fox, 1983

The spirit is something you can't hardly explain. The feeling of the spirit of the Lord can't be explained without you having the spirit in your soul. It is a good feeling—it's a feeling too good to explain! Just like in heaven, you can't even wash the spirit of the Lord out of your hands. The spirit is something great. I've had the spirit in my arms, in my whole body. I've had it so much, I feel so weak I could fall out. I have to sit down sometimes. I feel so weak in the Lord—I'm in the spirit! If you understand the spirit of the Lord, it's not weakness or sickness but meekness in the spirit.

GRACIE HOLLAND

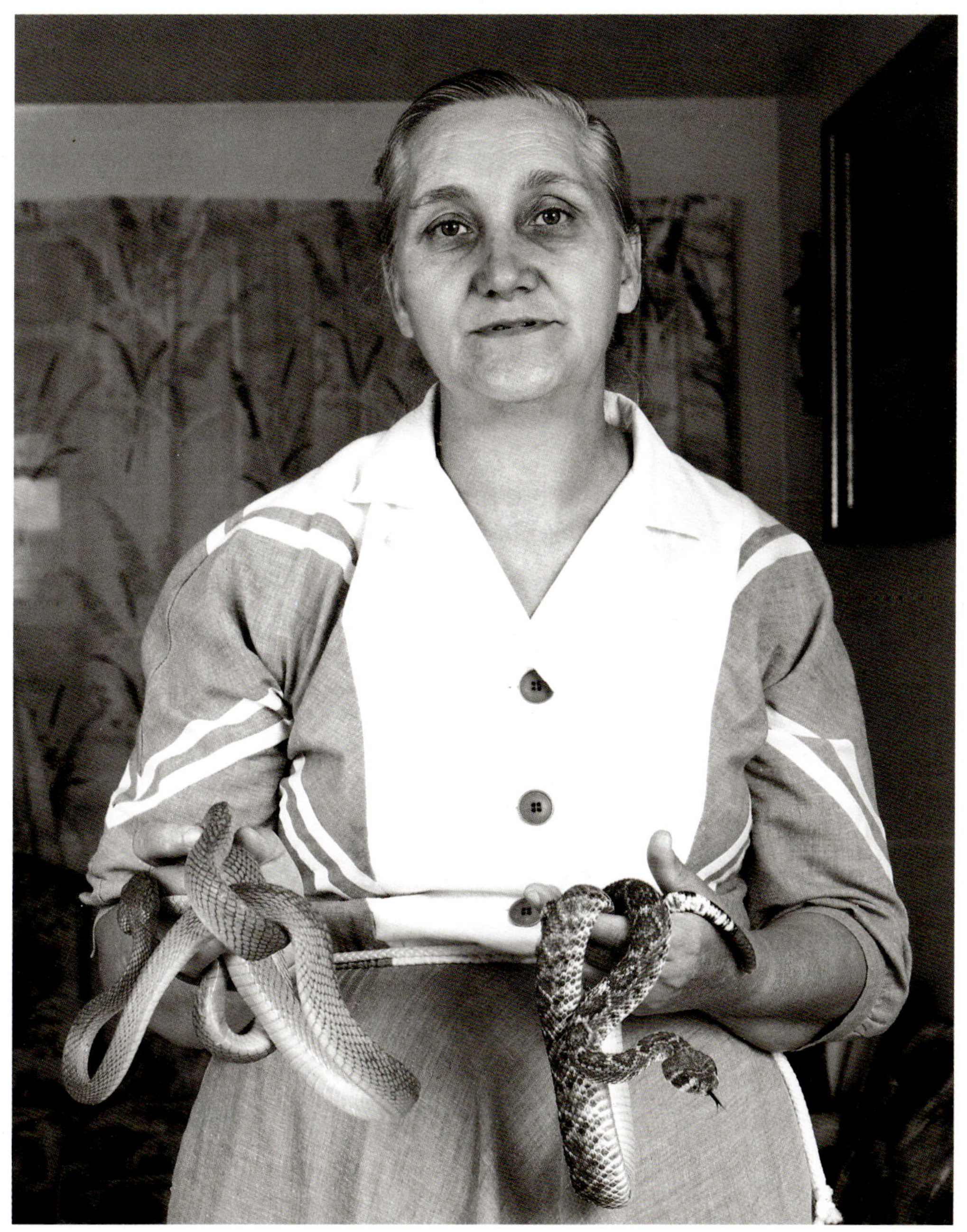

Gracie Serpent Handling, Happy, 1986

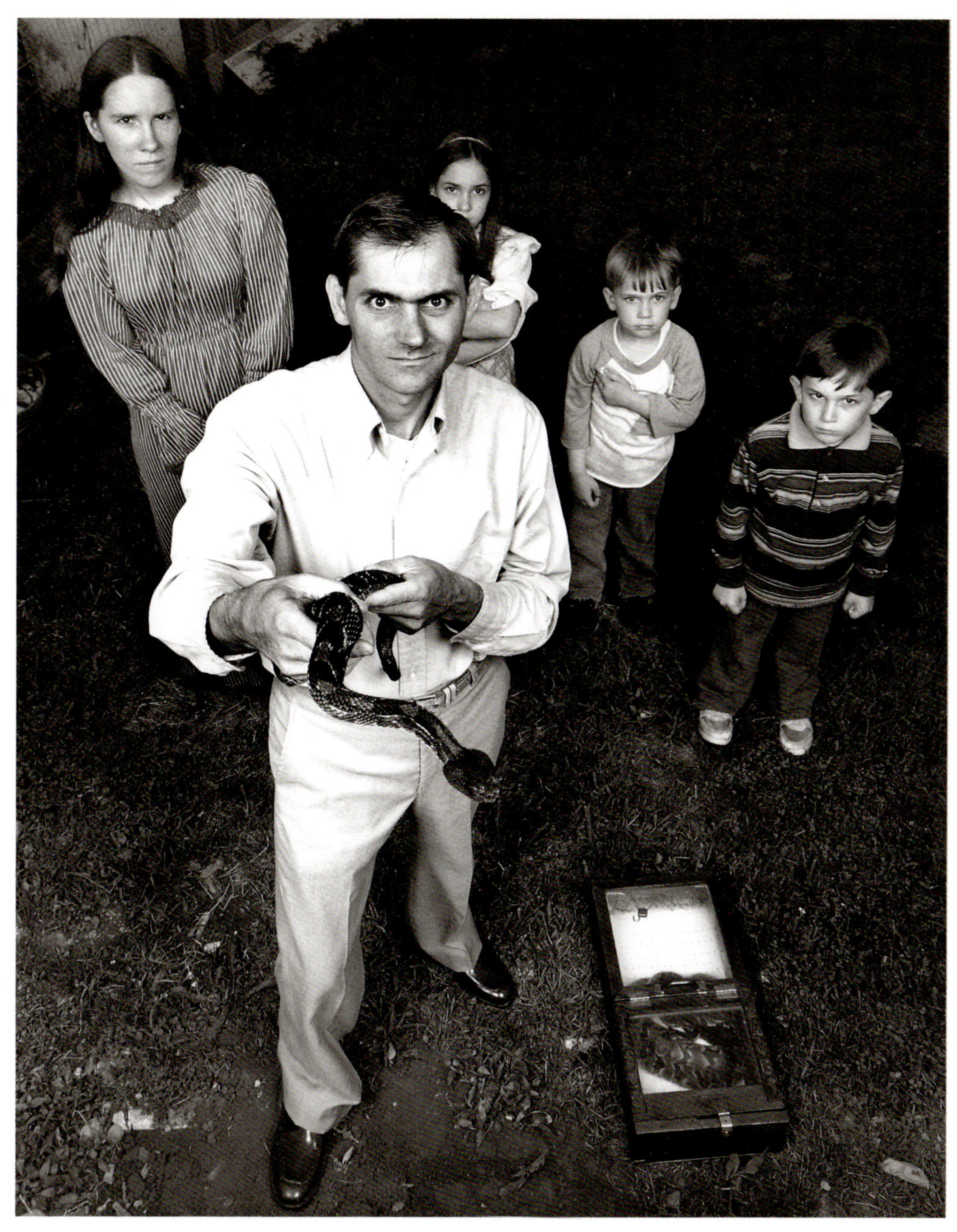

Holiness Man with Family, Jolo, W. Virginia, 1987

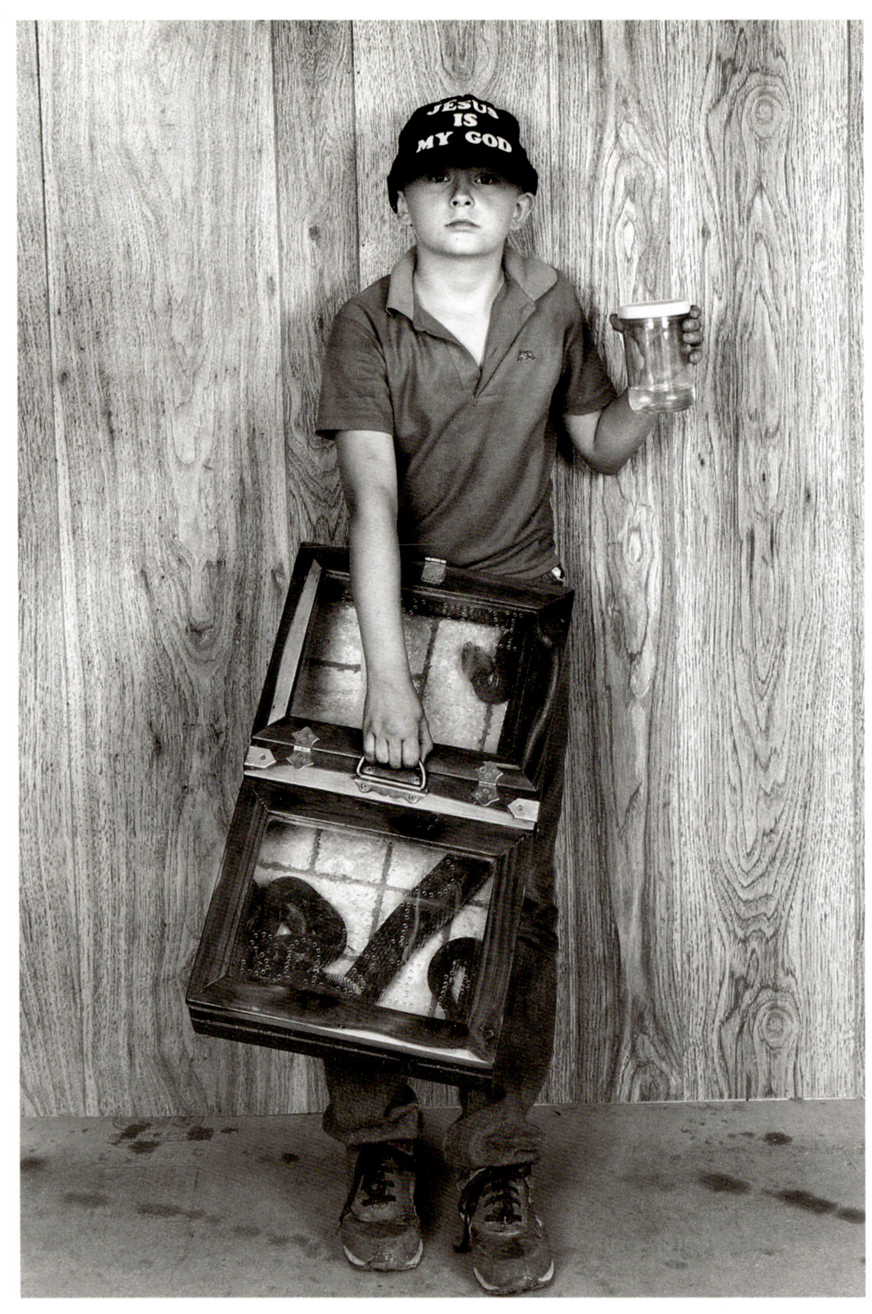

Holiness Boy with Serpent Box and Poison Jar, Harlan County, 1987

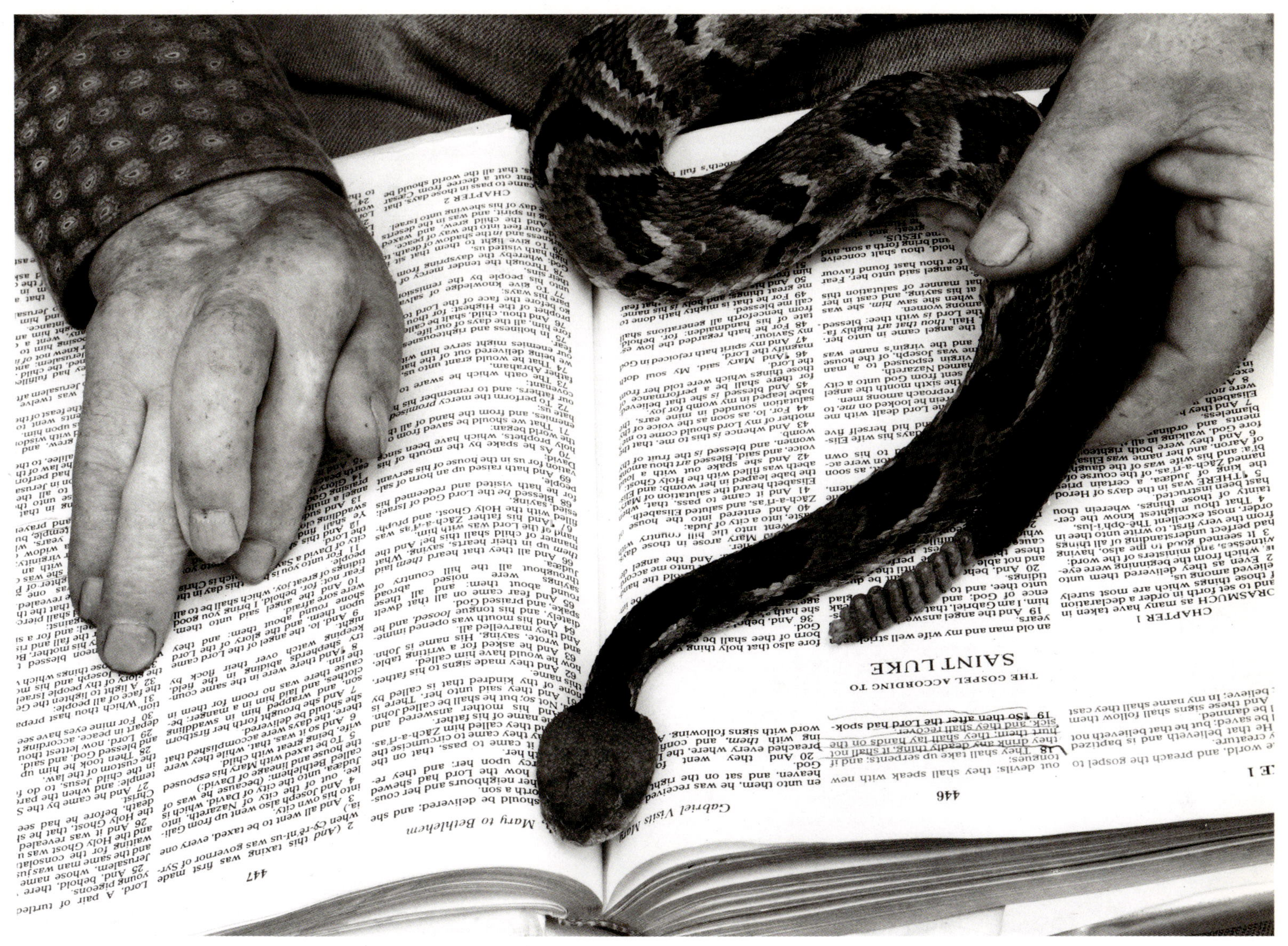

Holiness Hands with Serpent and Bible, Happy, 1987

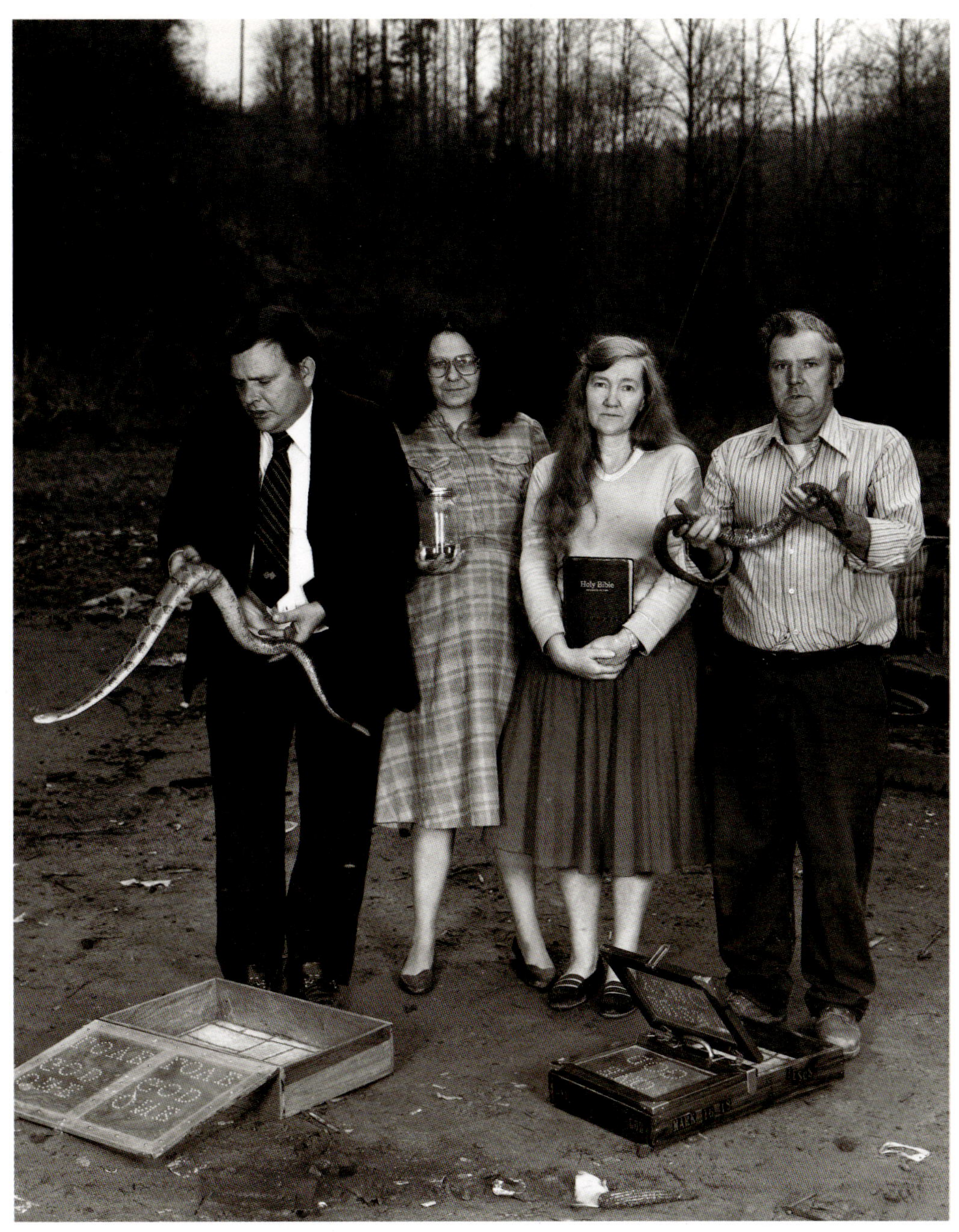

The Holiness Gathering, Beech Fork, 1987

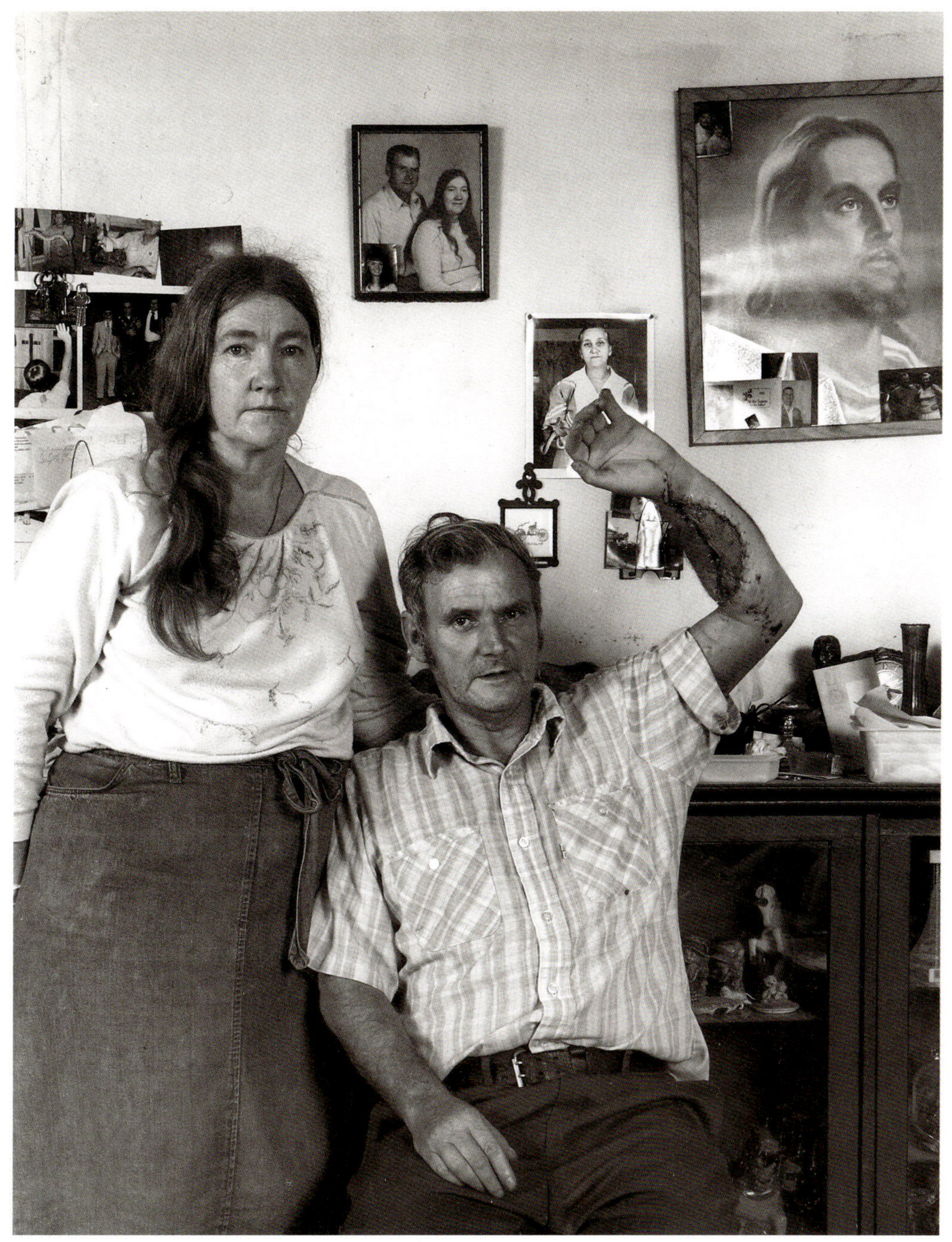

Wayne's Serpent Bite, Leatherwood, 1990

When thou walkest through the fire, thou shalt not be burned; neither shall the flame kindle upon thee.

ISAIAH 43:2

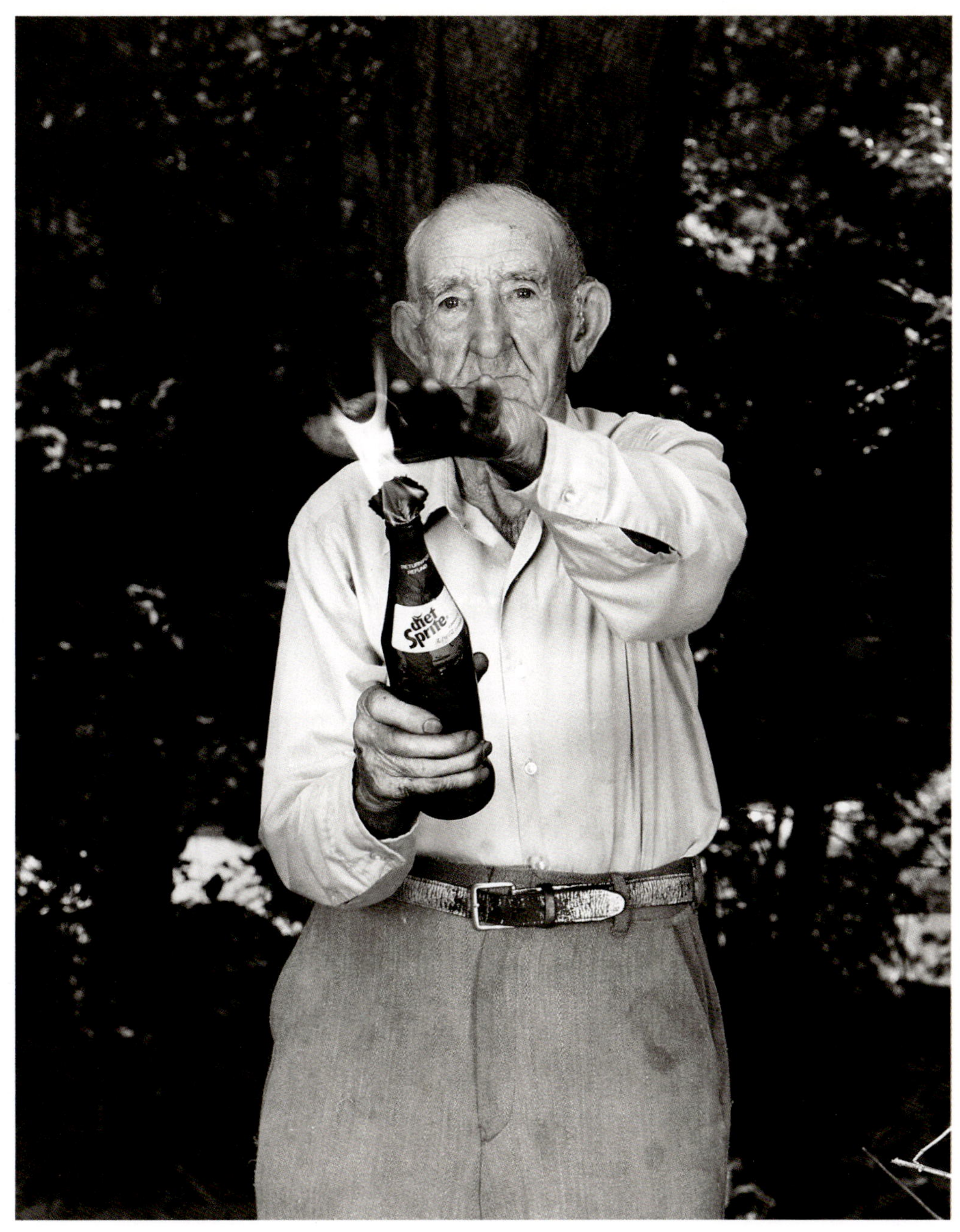

Brother Shell Firehandling, Harlan County, 1987

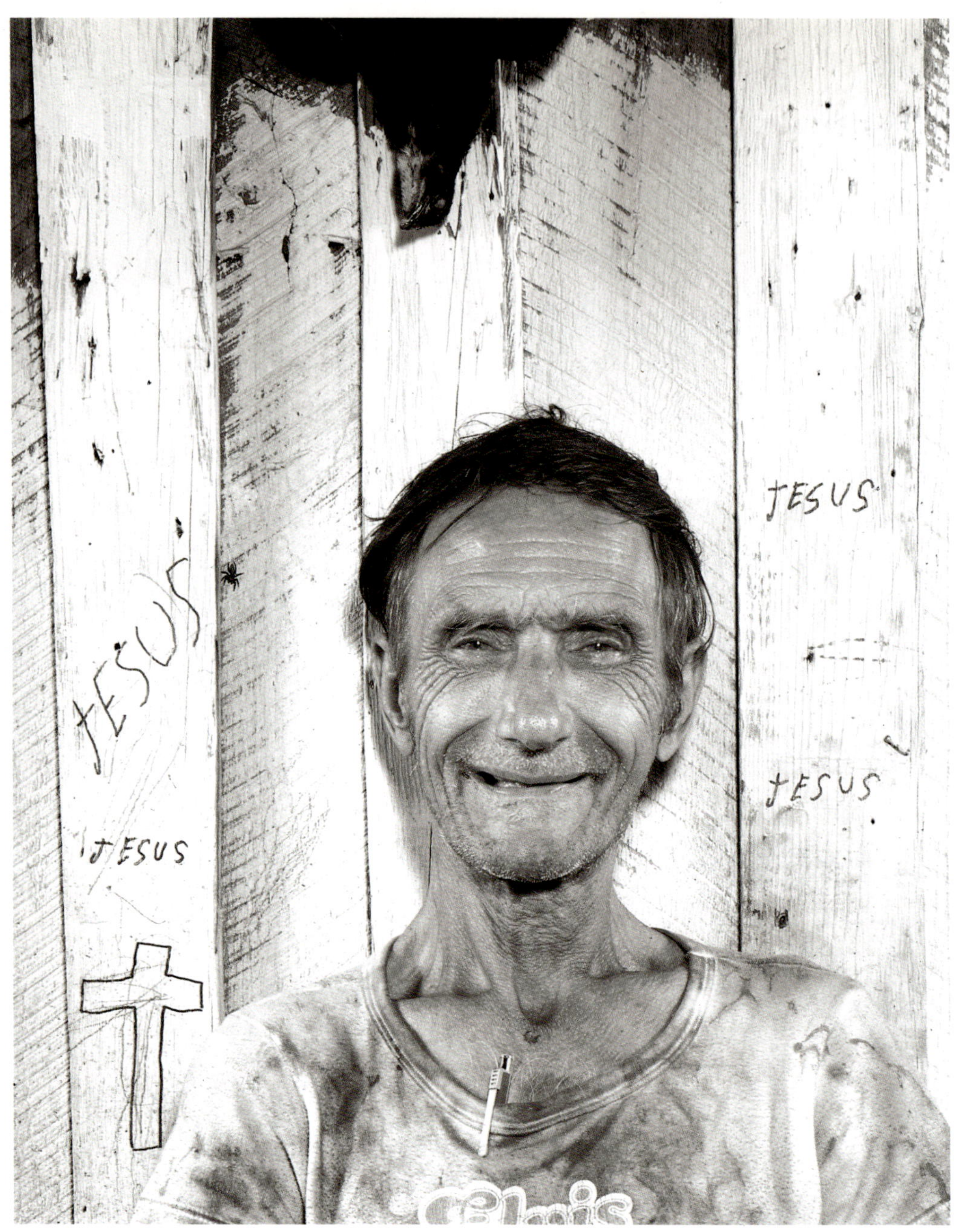

Hort with Chicken, Spider, Jesus and Elvis, Hooterville, 1992

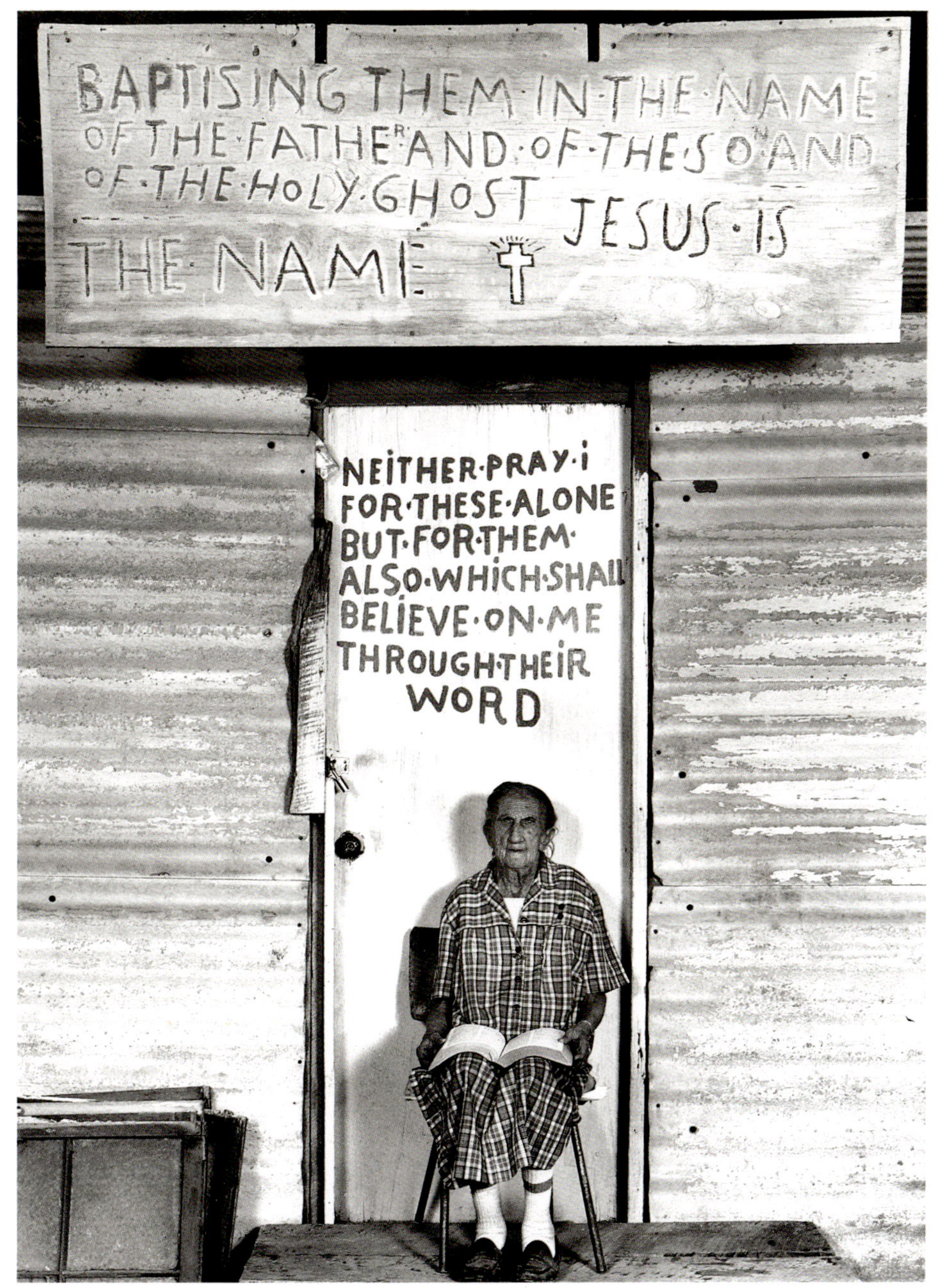

Baptizing Them, Hooterville, 1991

VISITS

The aim of every artist is to arrest motion, which is life, by artificial means and hold it fixed so that one hundred years later, when a stranger looks at it, it moves again, since it is life. Since man is mortal, the only immortality possible for him is to leave something behind him that is important, since it will always move.

William Faulkner

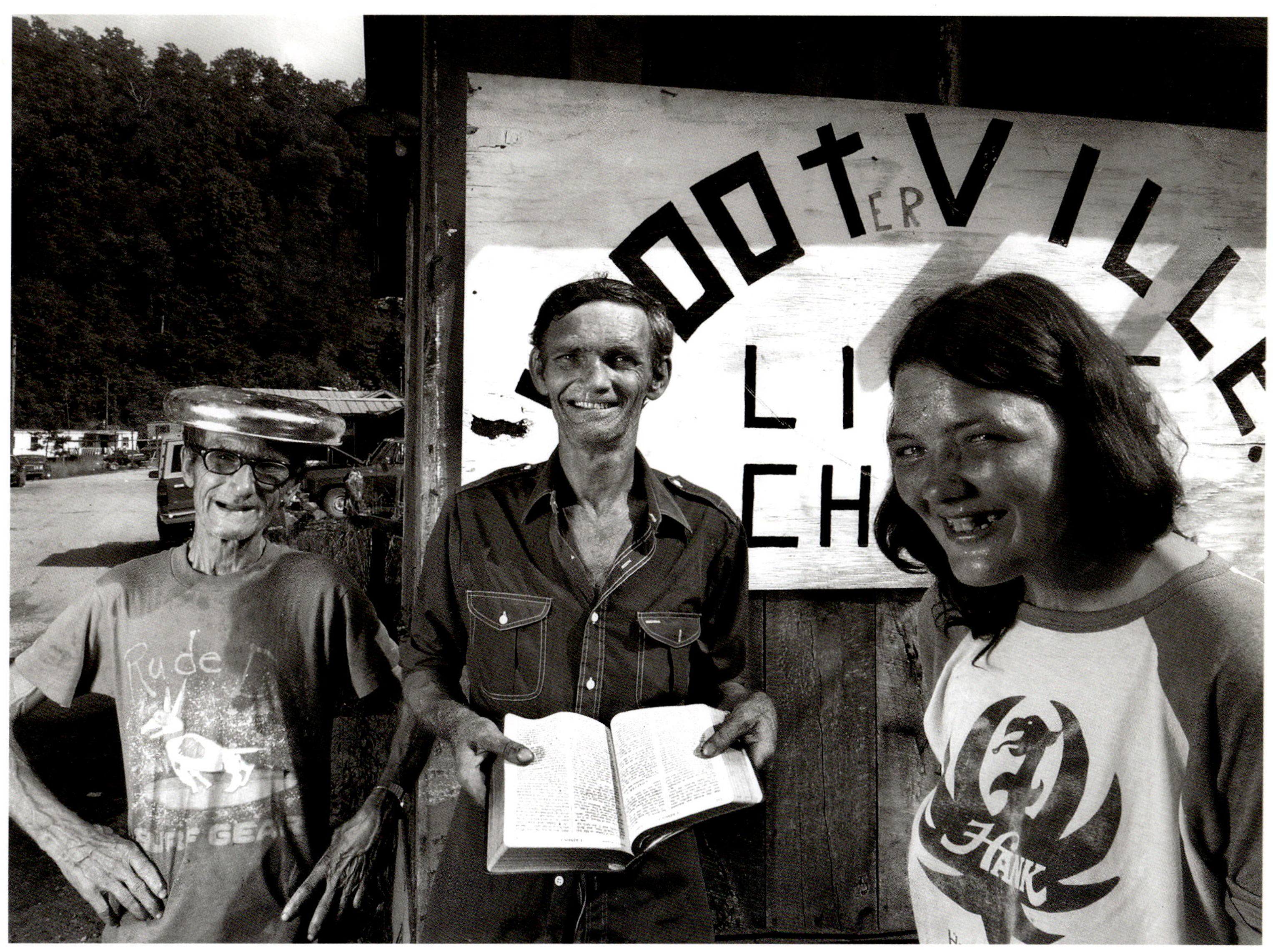

Hooterville Little Church, Hooterville, 1991

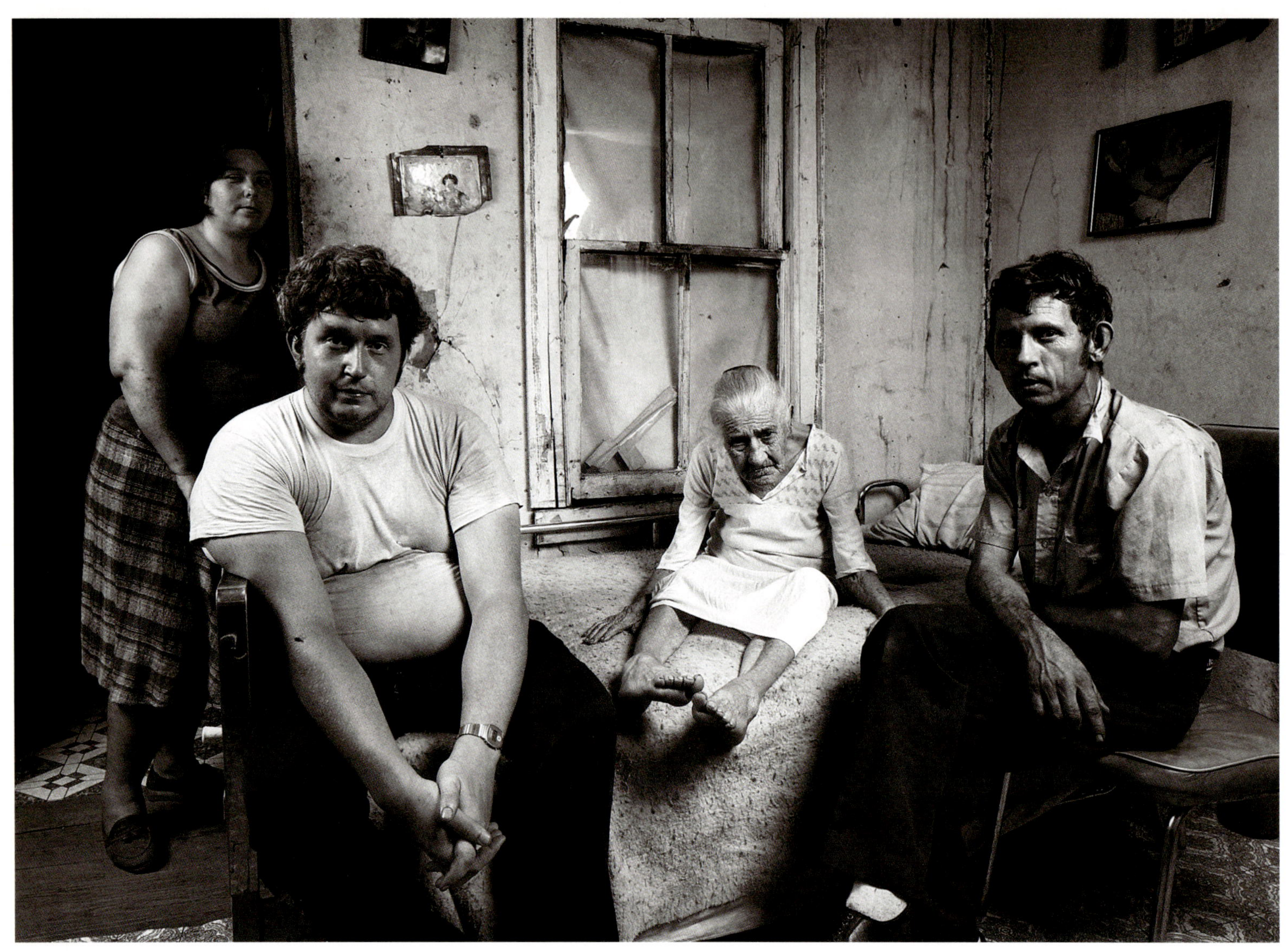

103-Year-Old Woman and Family, Neon, 1986

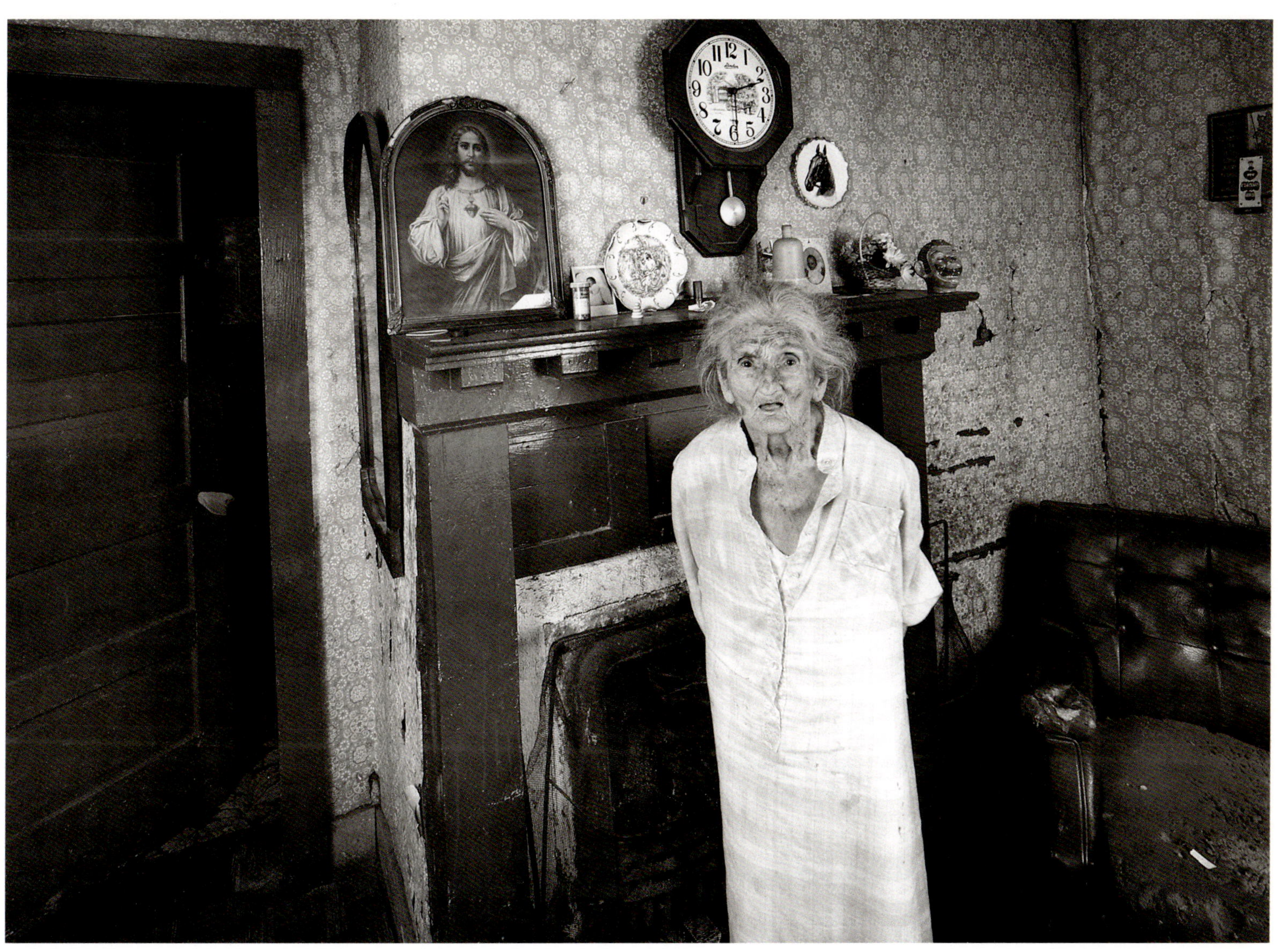

105-Year-Old Woman, Rocky Hollow, 1986

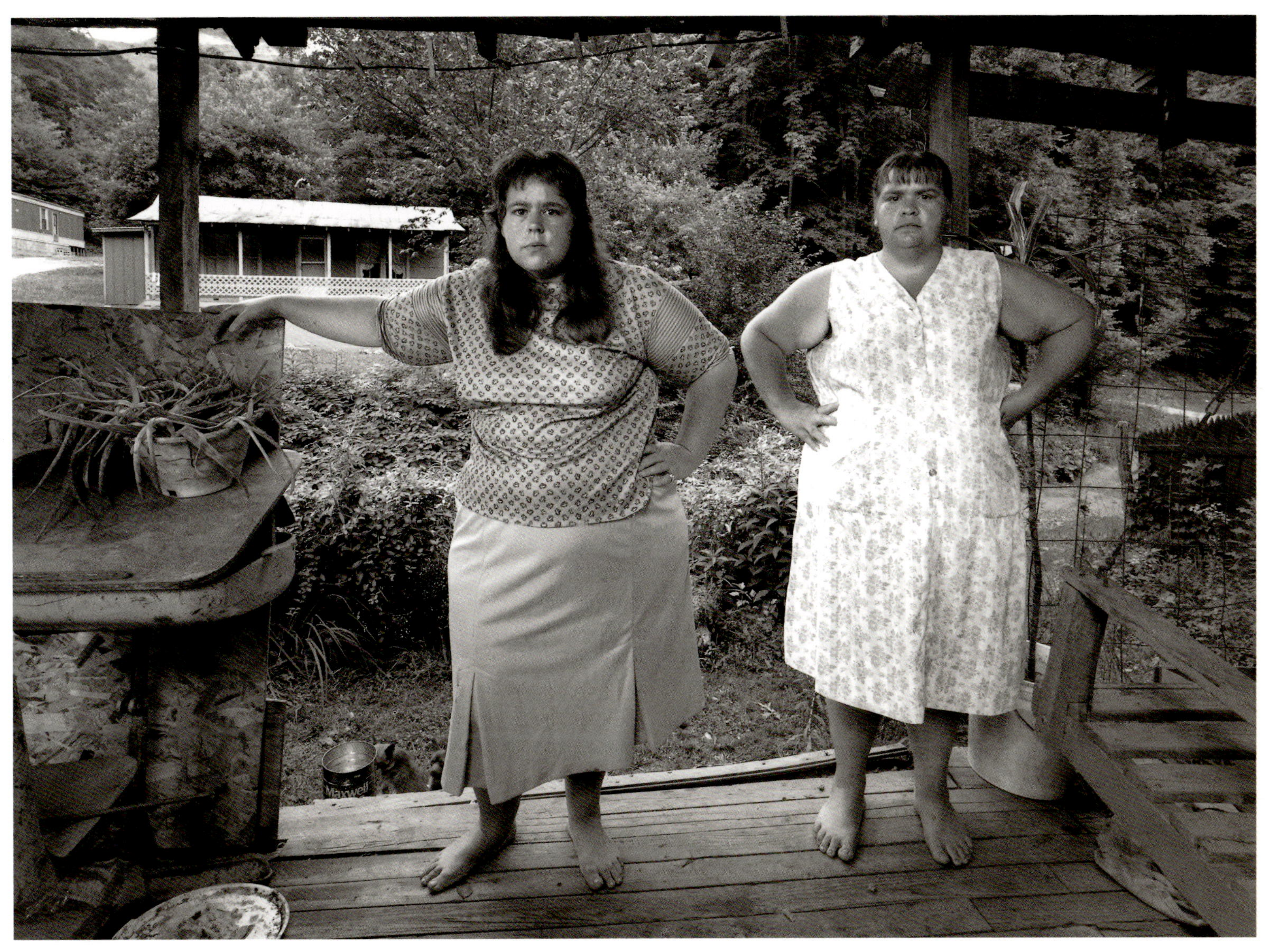

Mattie and Daisy, Camp Branch, 1989

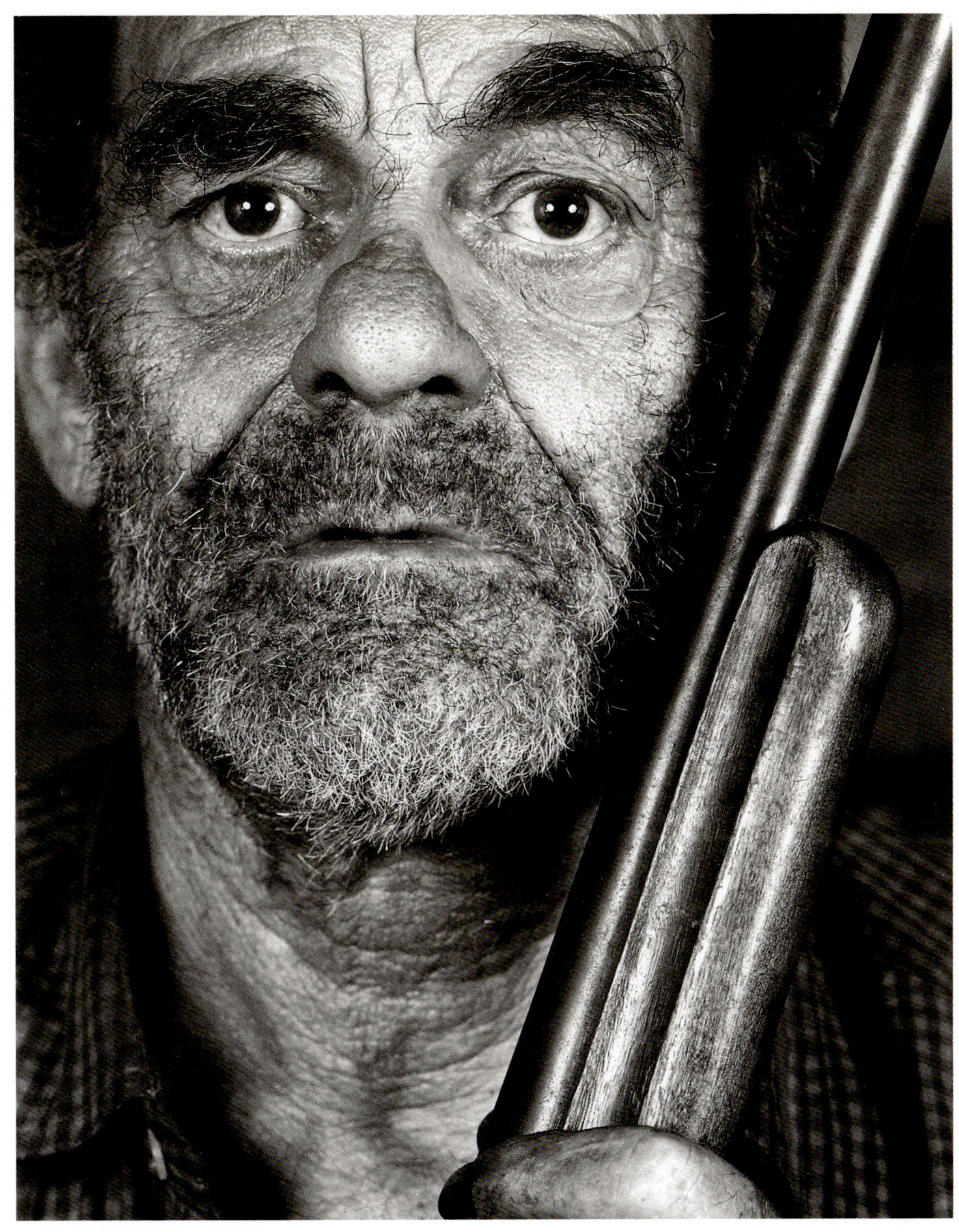

Jesse Estep, Harlan County, 1986

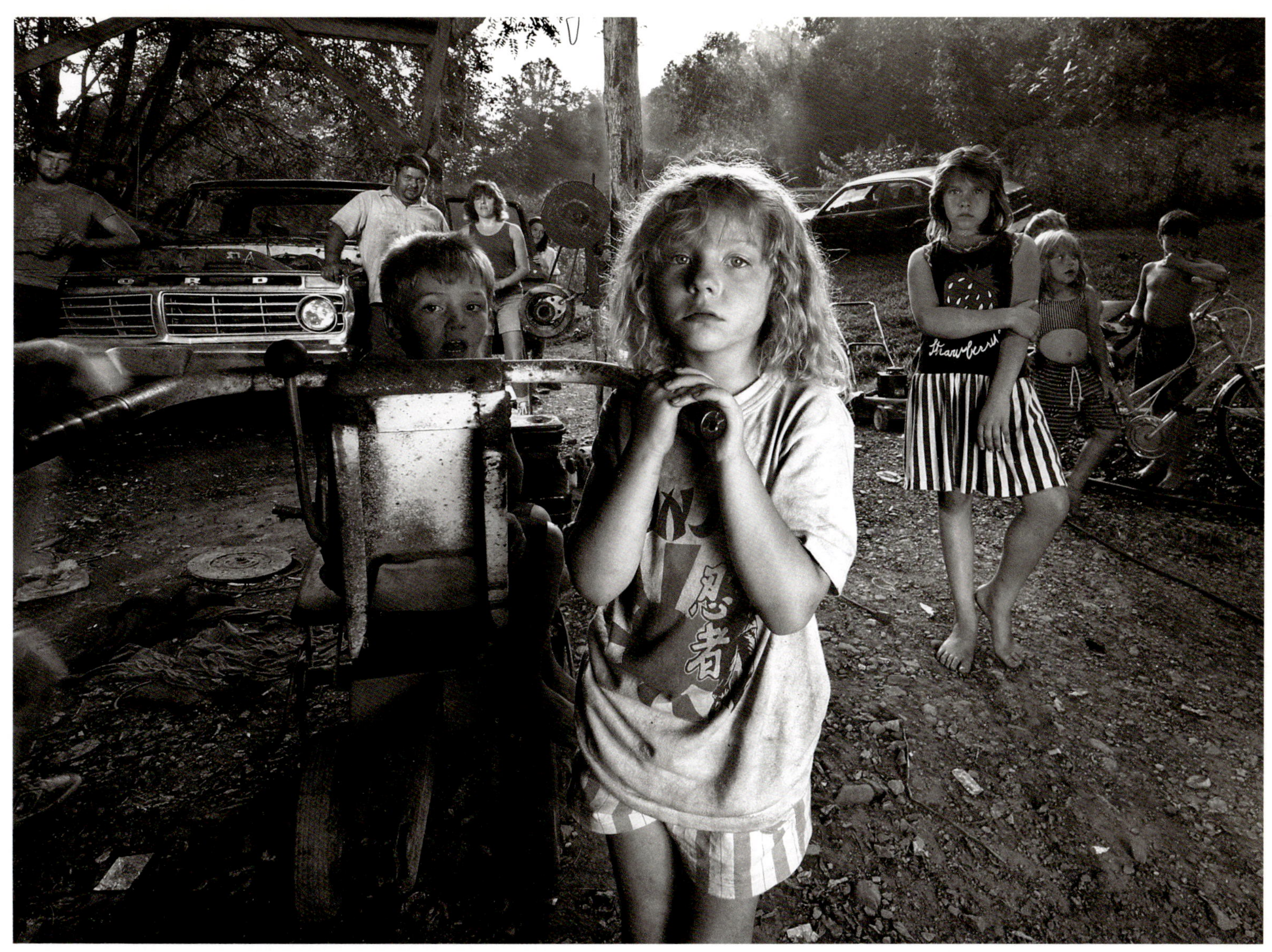

Children at Topmost, Topmost, 1991

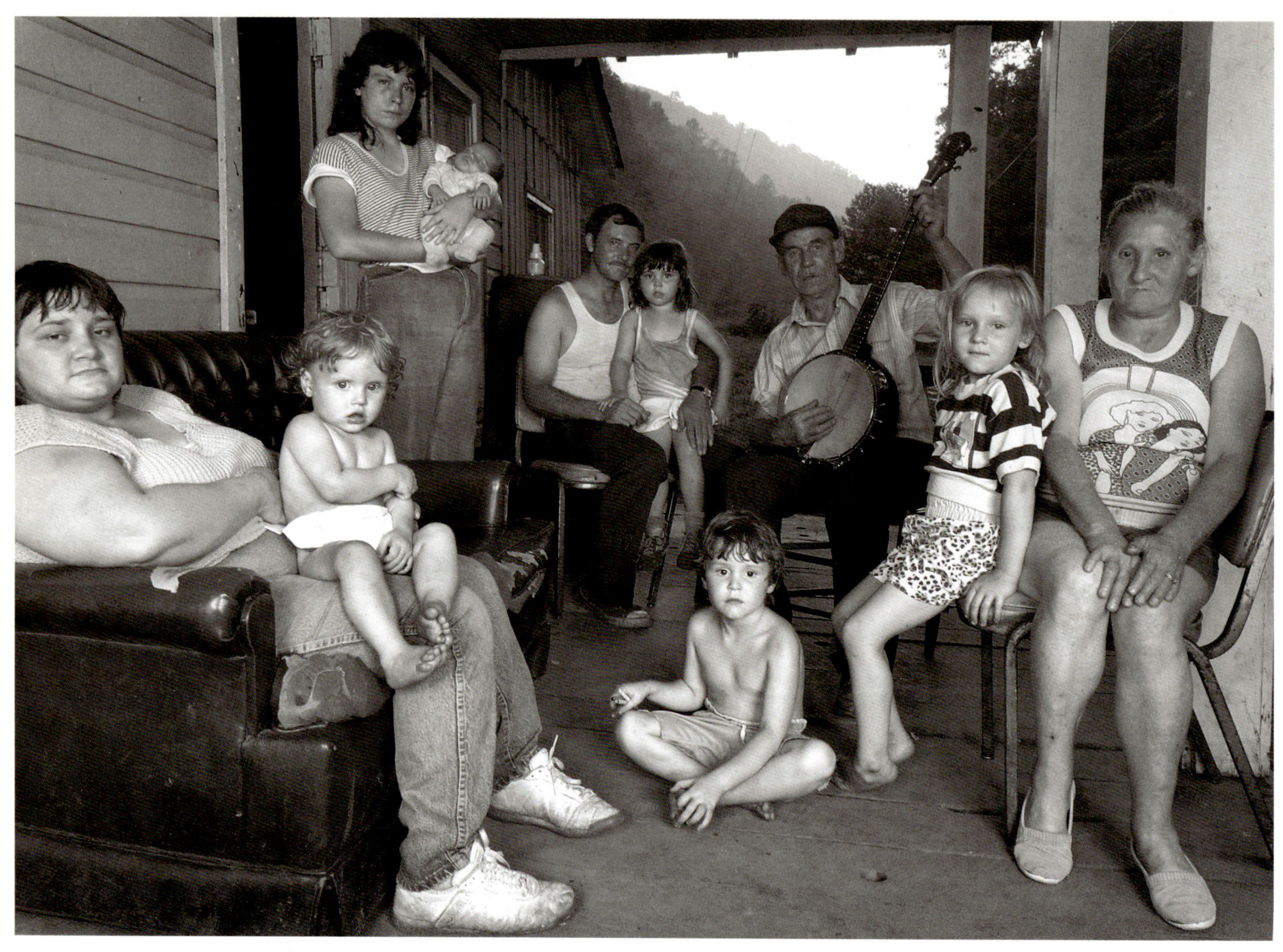

The Banks Family Porch, Punchin Camp, 1989

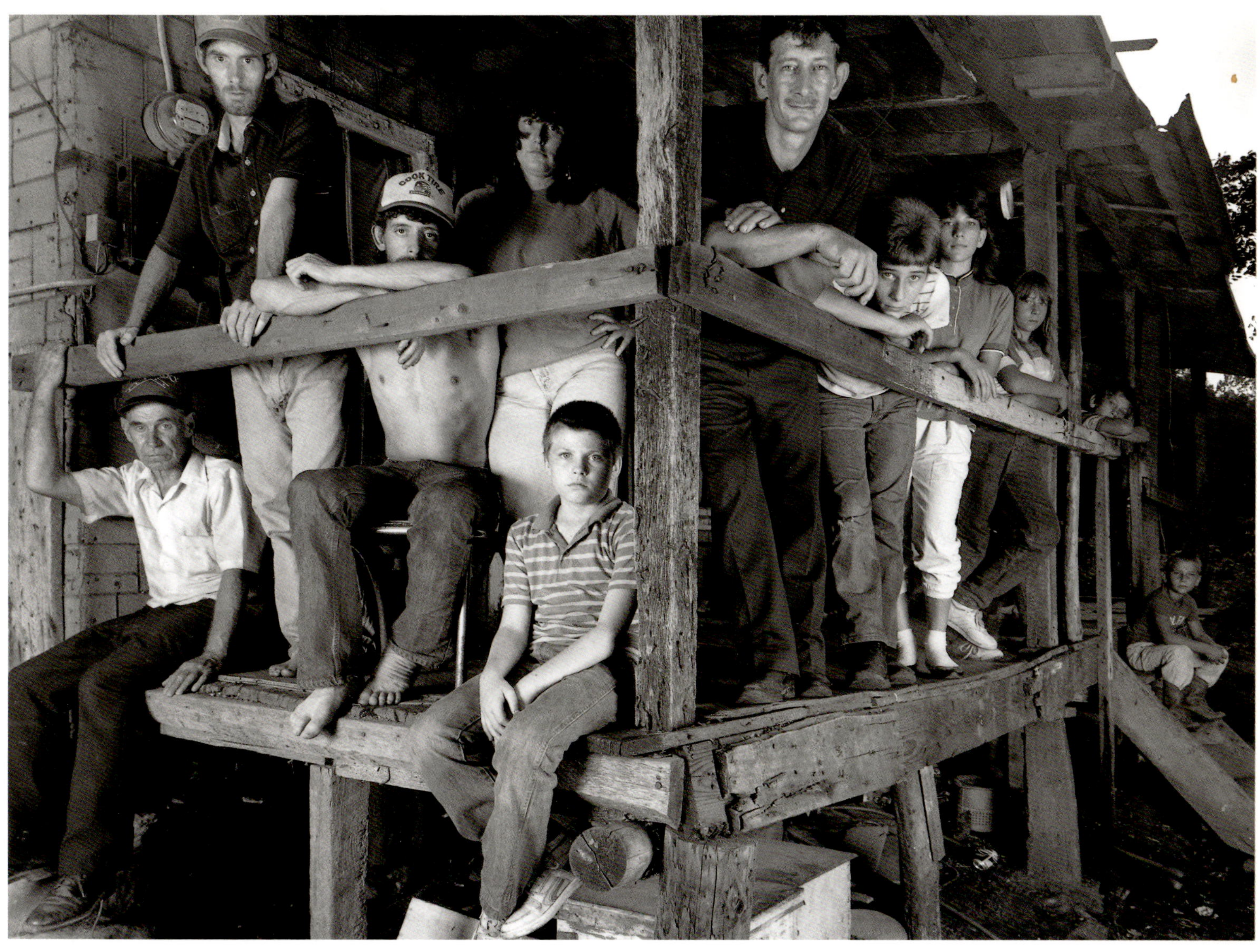

The Banks Family Porch, Beech Fork, 1987

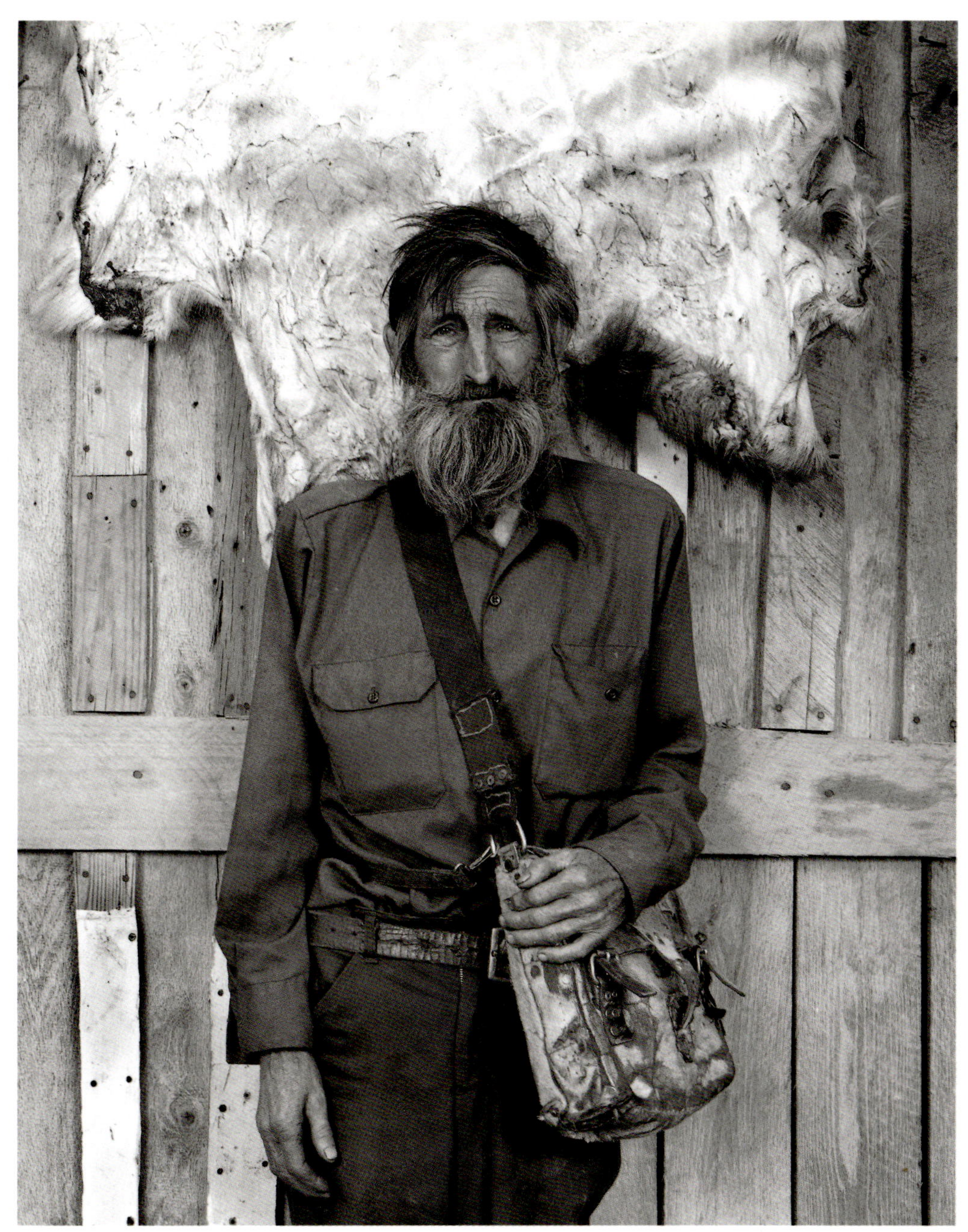

Ellis Bailey, Yeaddiss, 1989

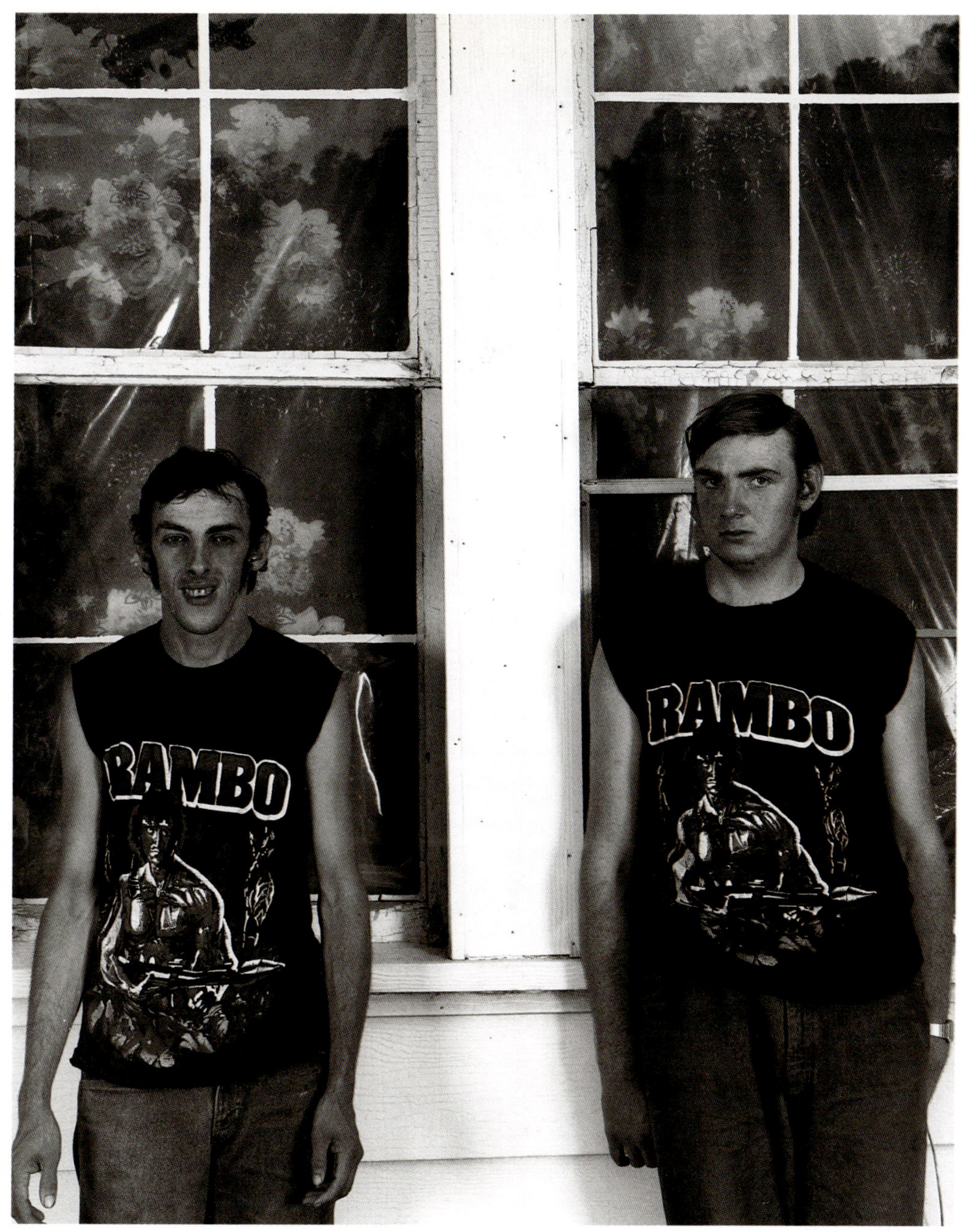

The Rambo Boys, Pistol City, 1987

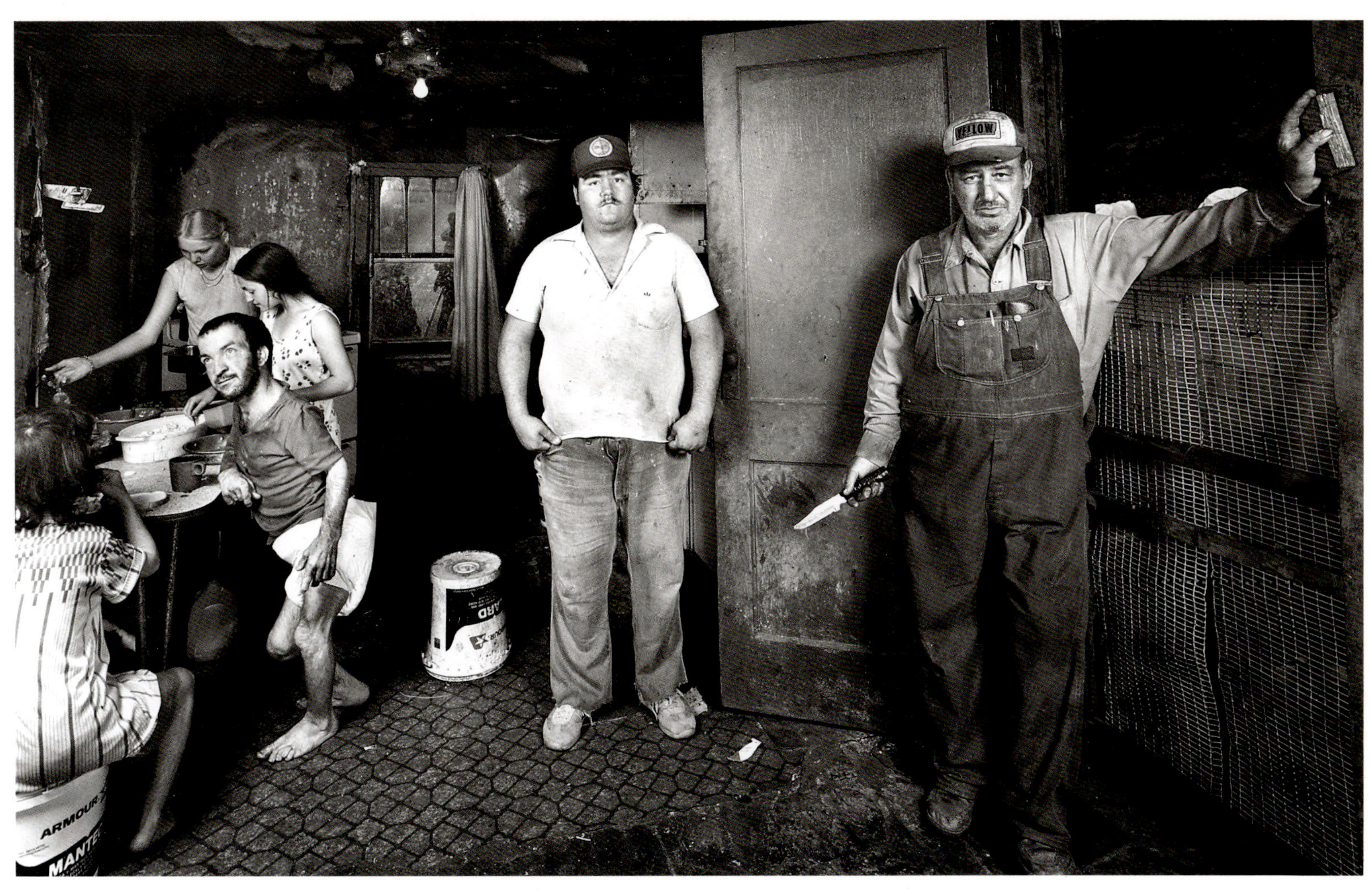

The Childers' Kitchen, Neeley Branch, 1986

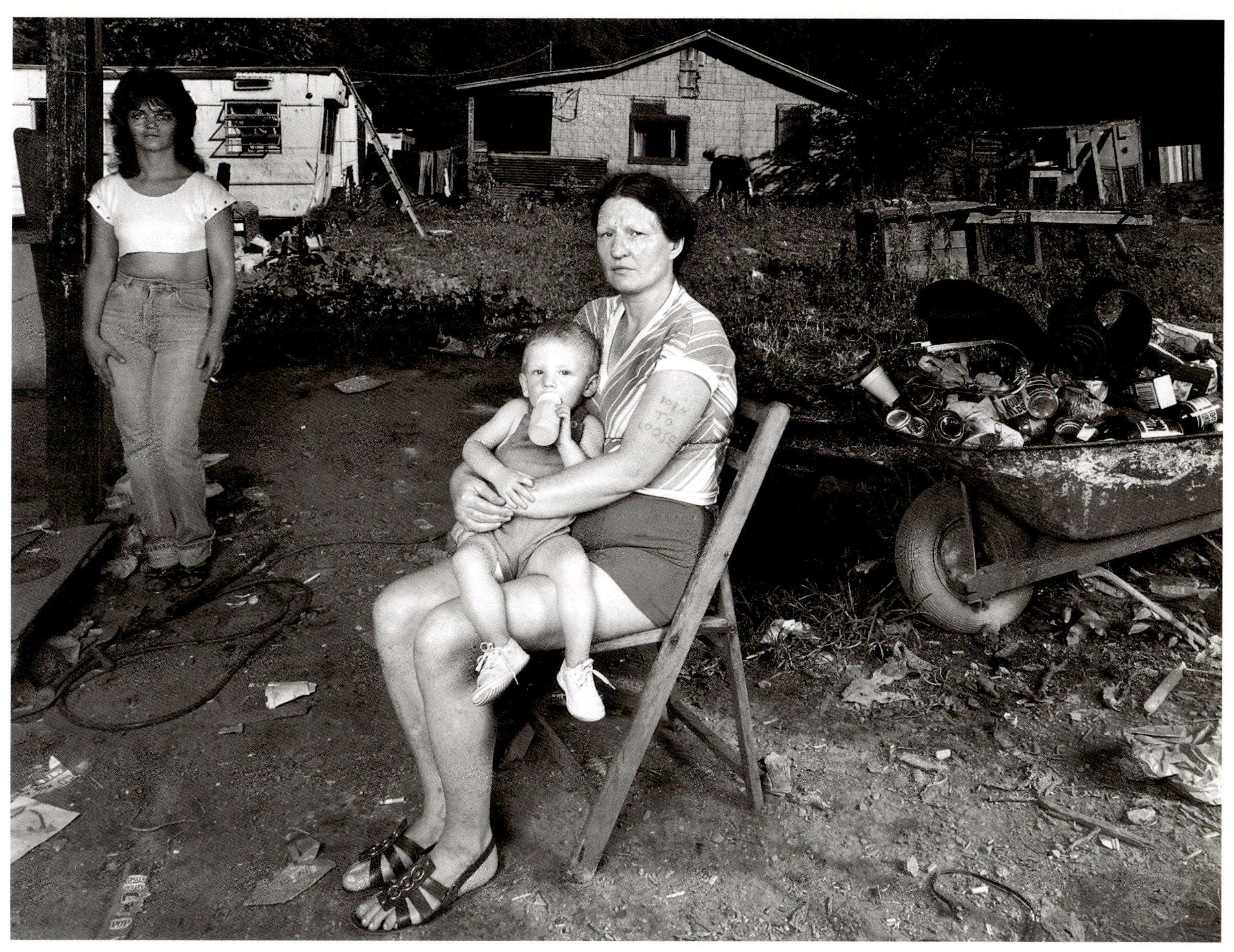

Born To Loose, Cannie Creek, 1987

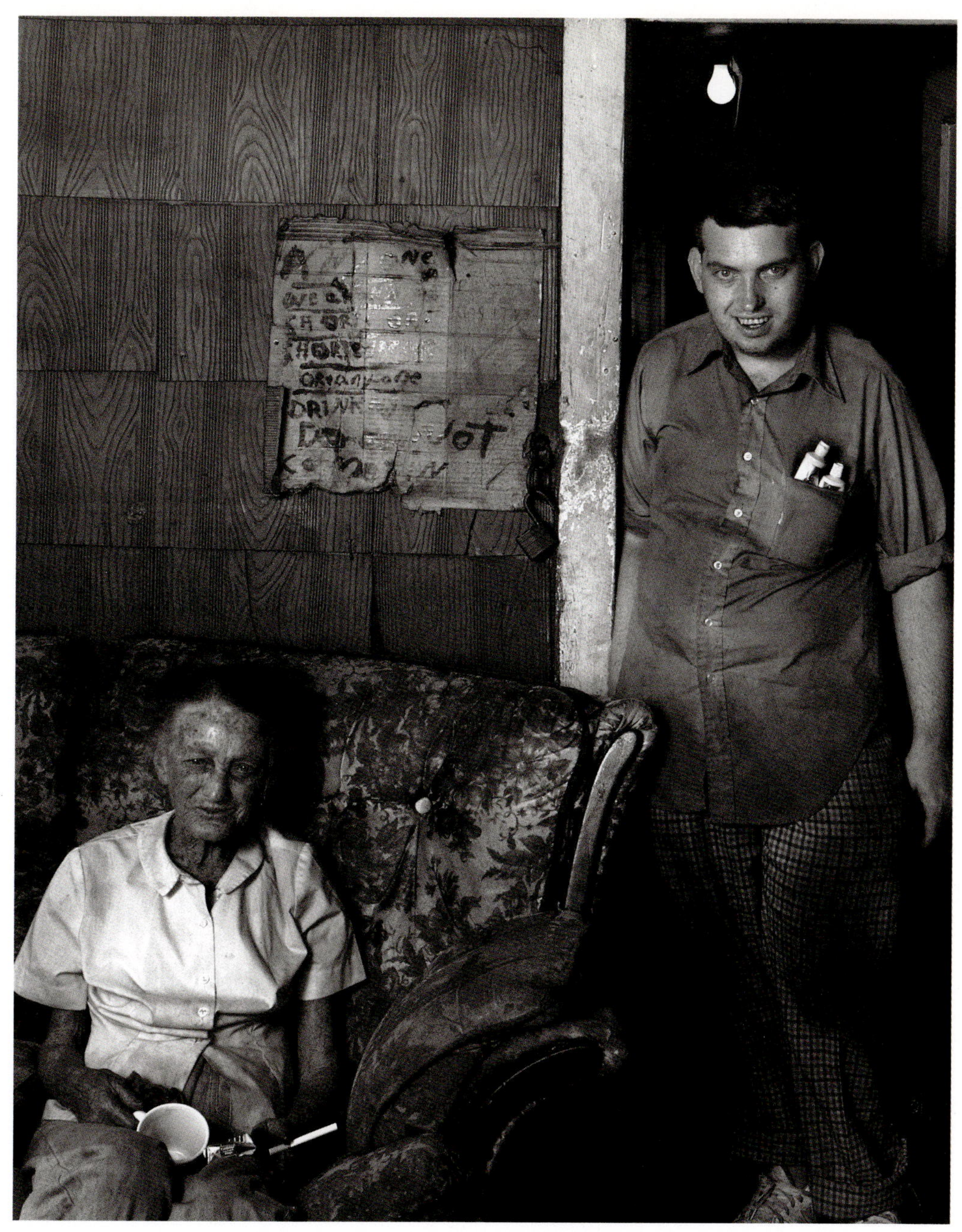

Do Not Come In, Delphia, 1989

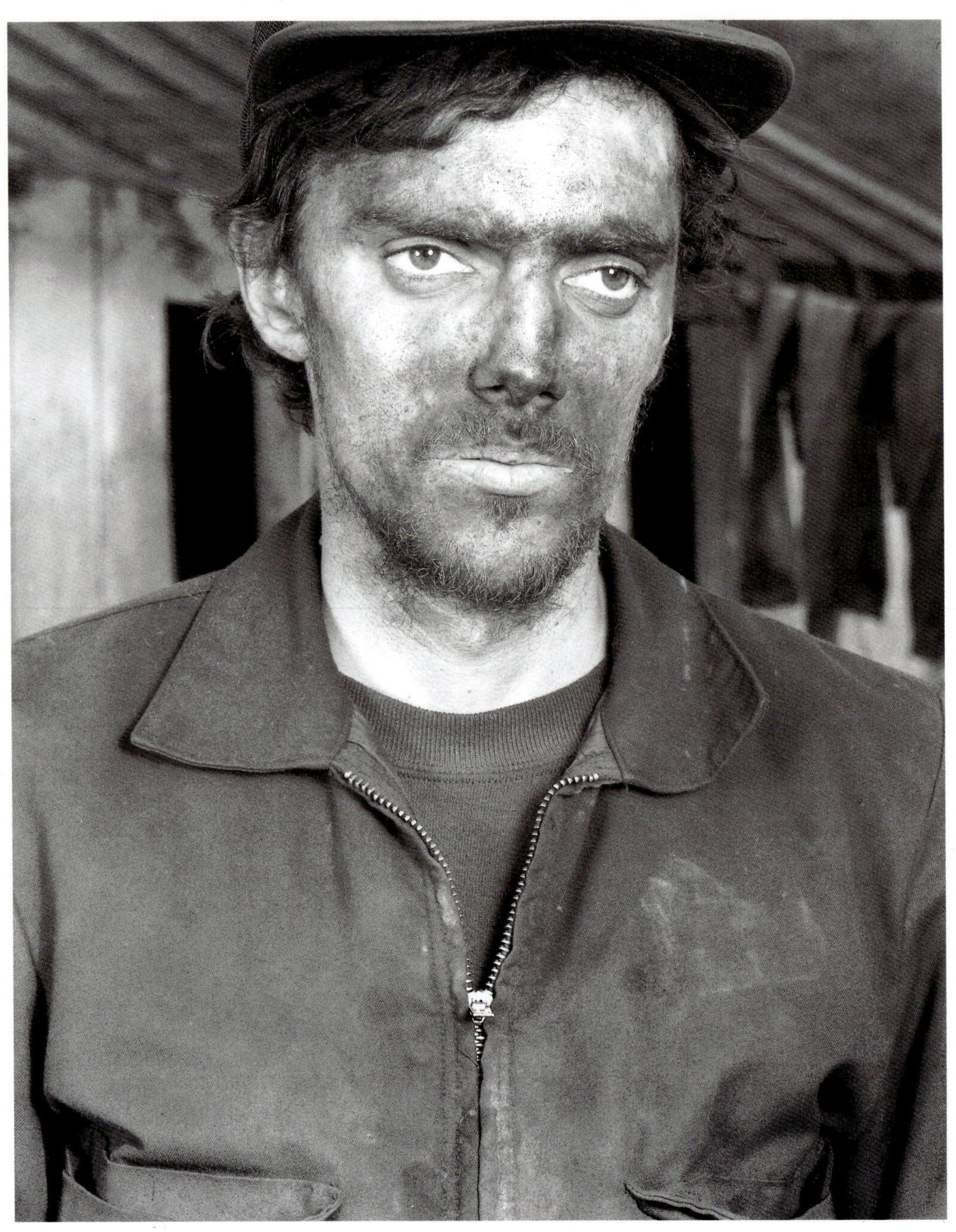

The Coal Miner, Isom, 1988

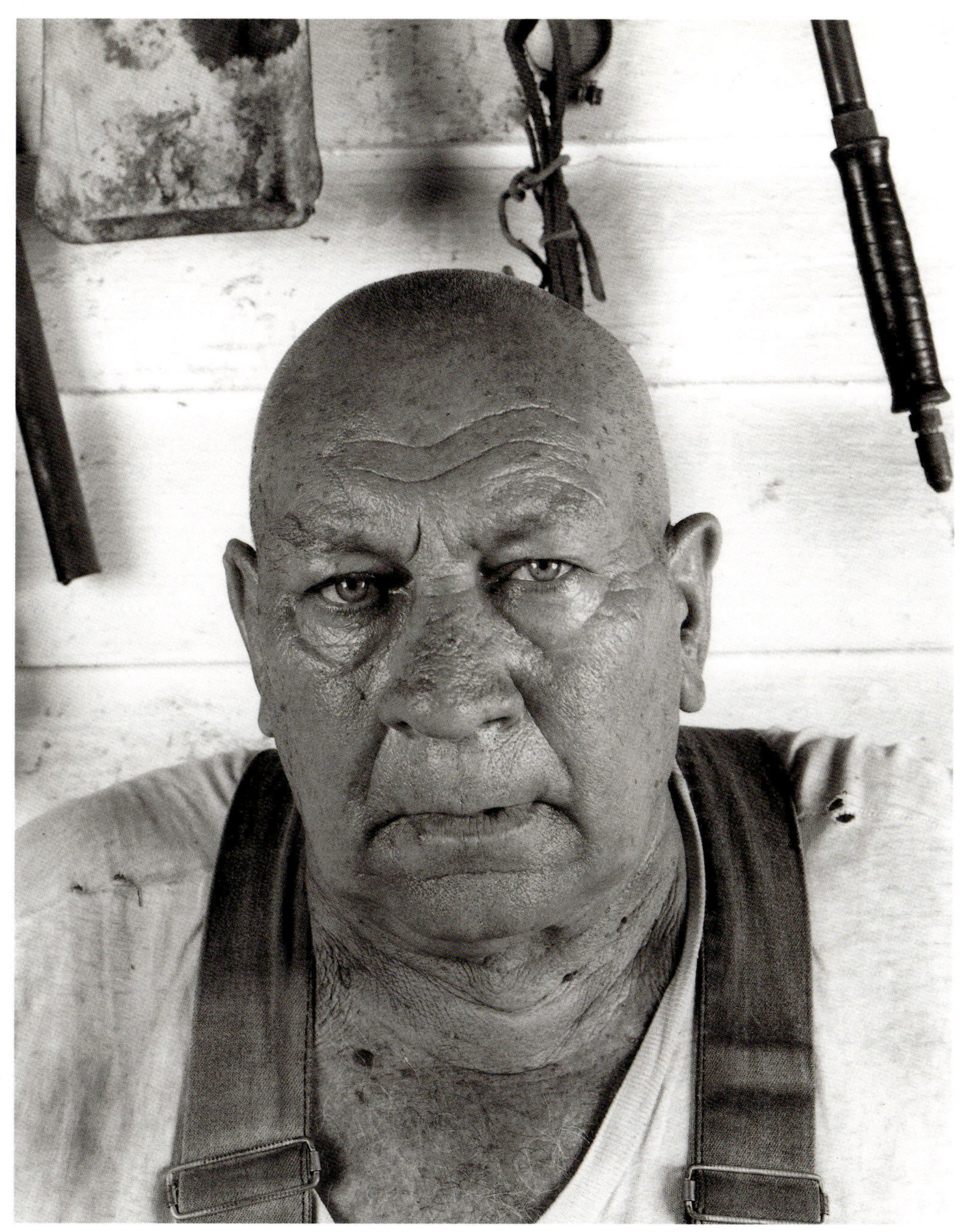

Hooch-a-pap, Beech Fork, 1987

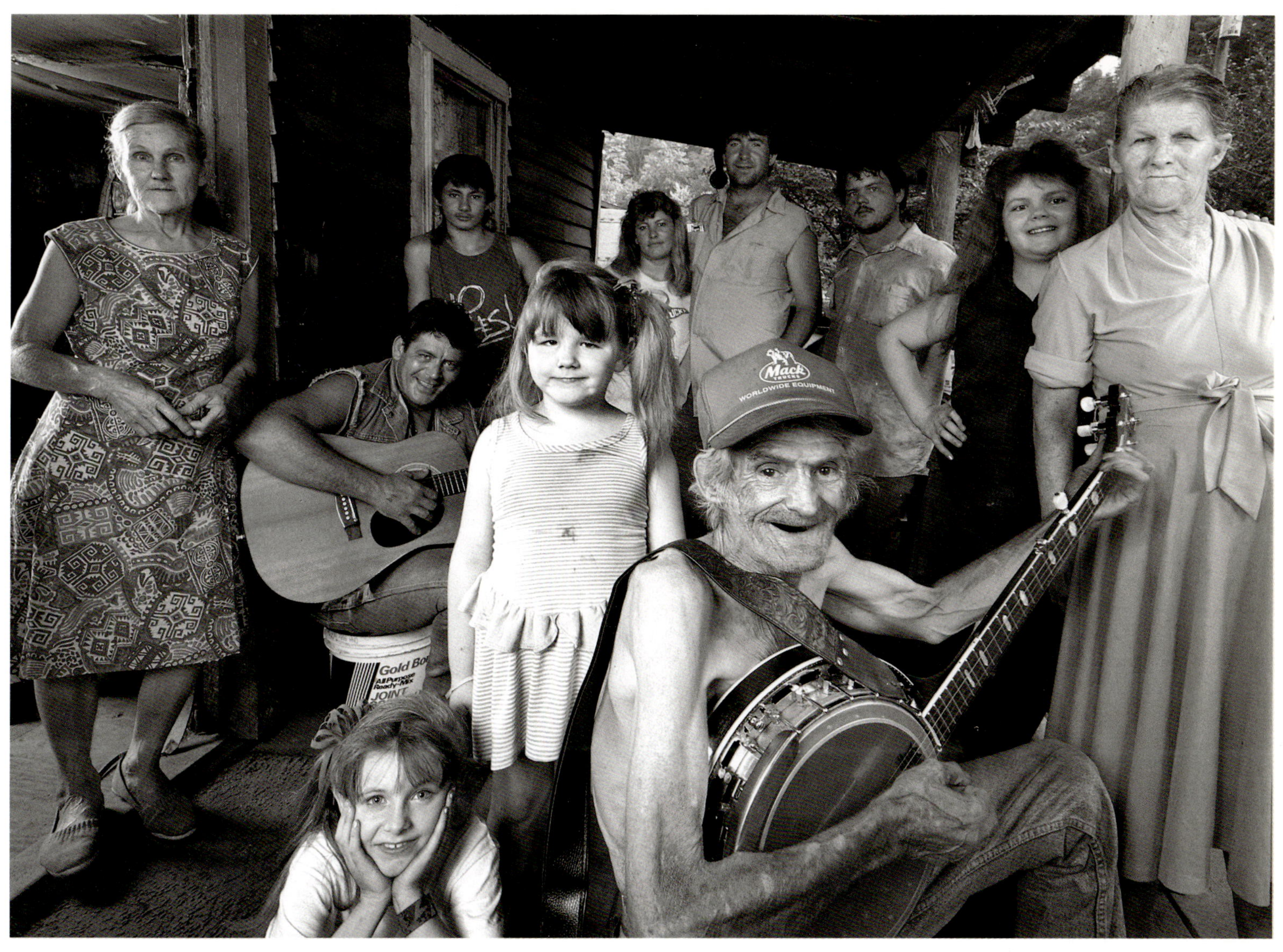

George's Branch Porch, George's Branch, 1991

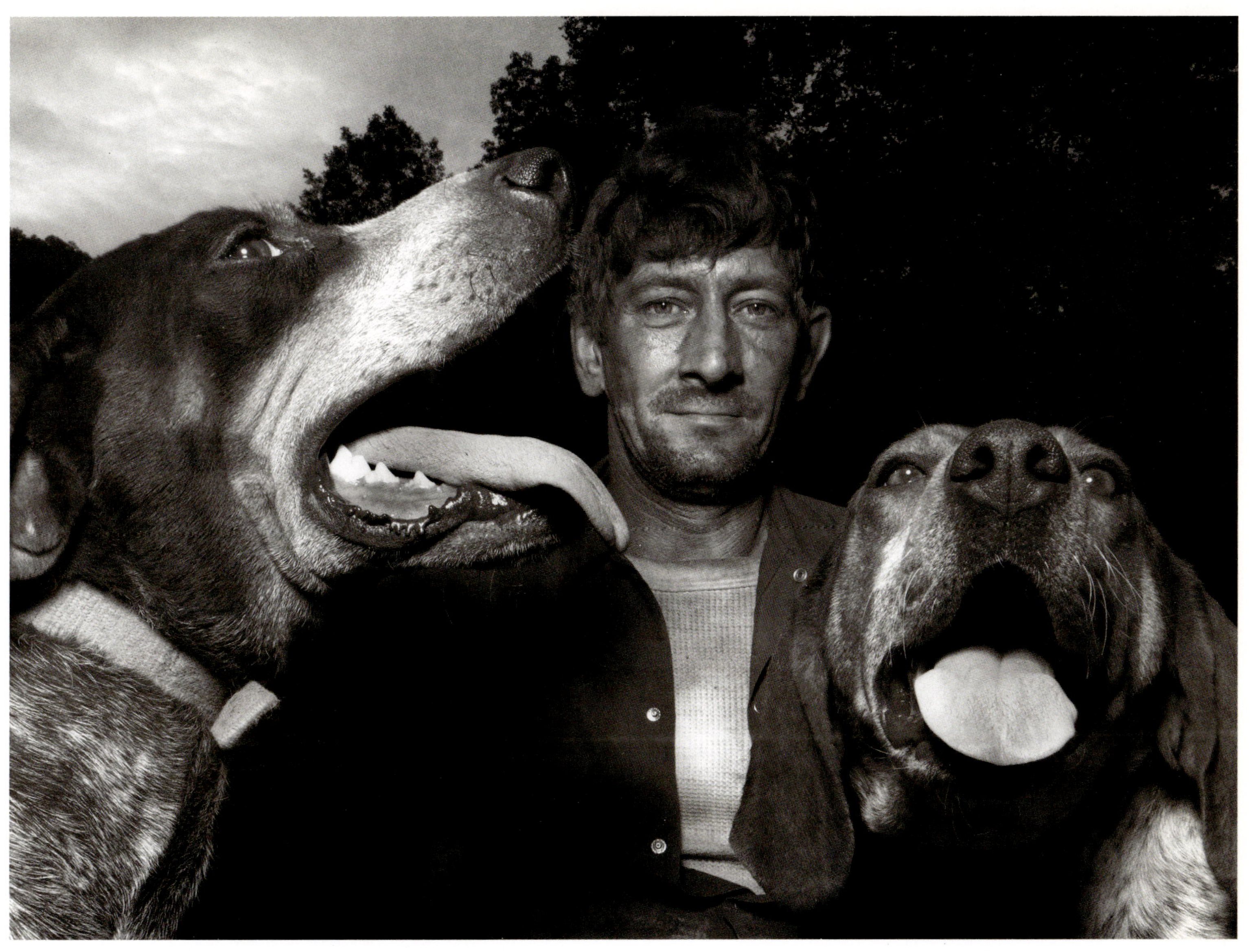

Chester and His Hounds, Delphia, 1992

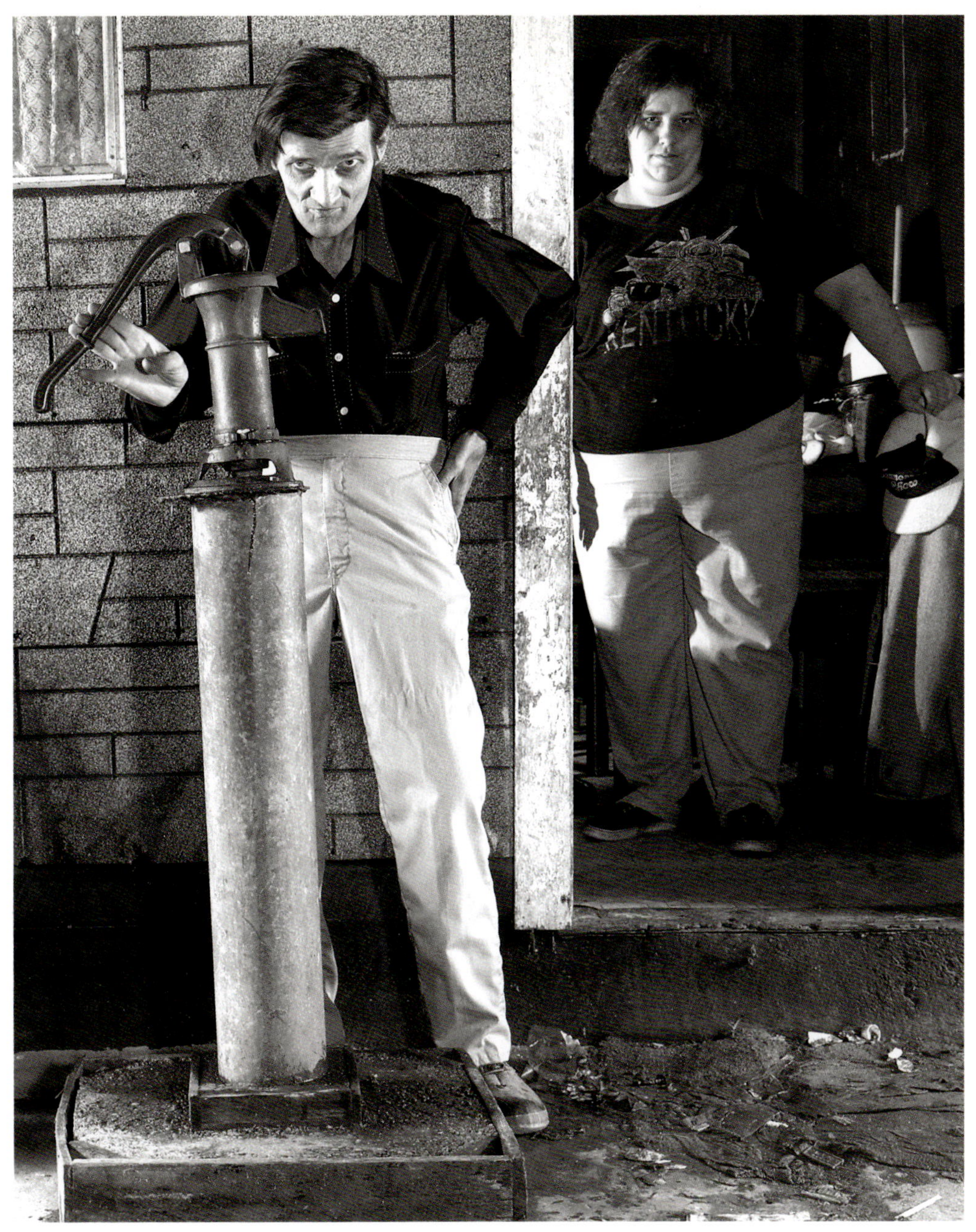

Harlan and Cathy with Water Pump, Cannie Creek, 1992

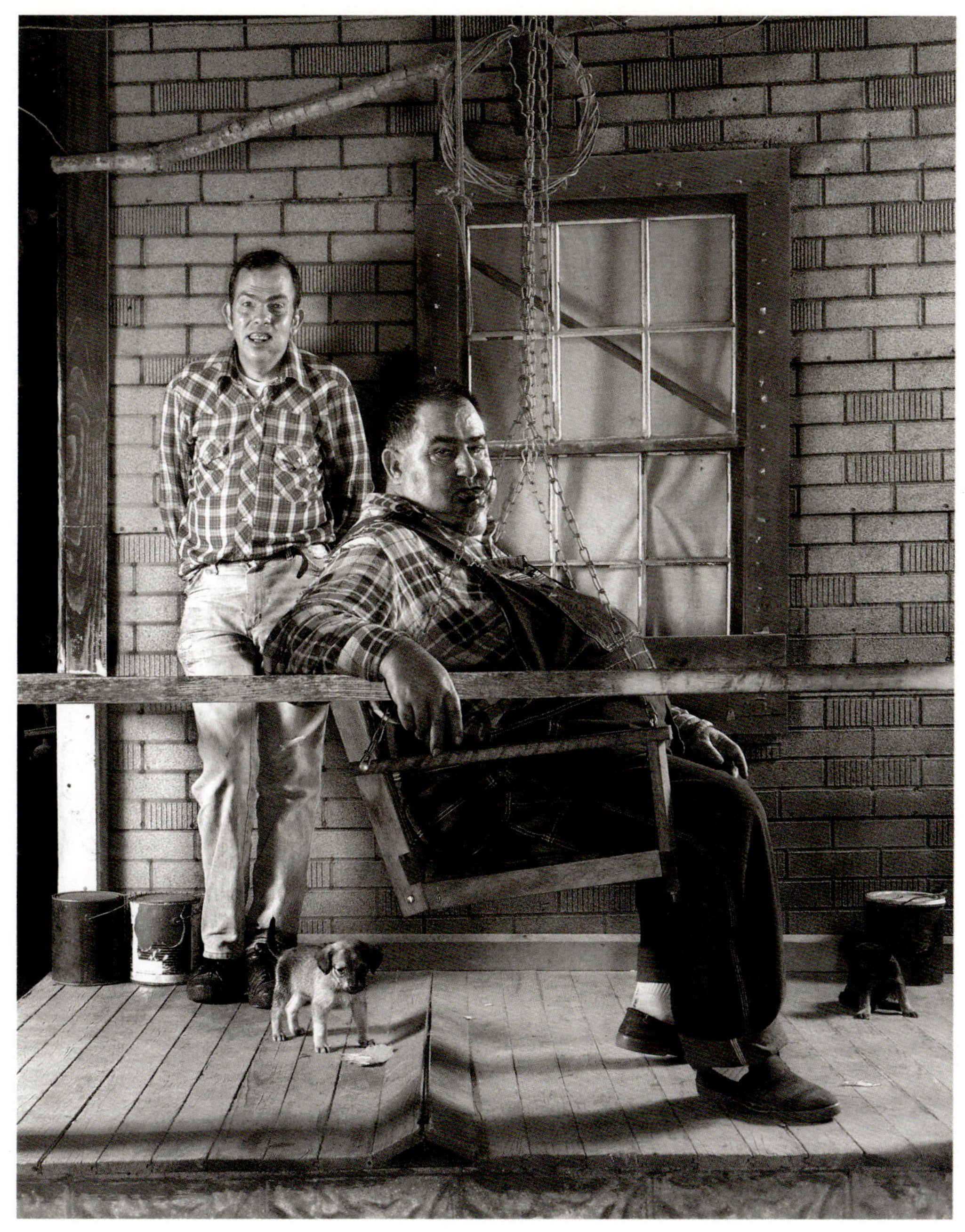

Brice and Crow on Porch, Buck Lick, 1992

ACKNOWLEDGMENTS

This work is the result of the patience, generosity and commitment of many people. First and foremost, I wish to thank the Appalachian people themselves who have given time and assistance to me over the years. Their open acceptance of me has deeply enriched my life. Wayne and Ratchel Riddle, Roy Banks, Hort Collins, Larry Craft, Chester Spencer, Ralph Mullins, and Junior Childers are just a few of the people who have traveled with me thousands of miles to introduce me to families and help in the making of these photographs.

Over the years I have valued the friendship and continued interest of a few artists whose encouragement has enriched this work. They are Eldred P. Davis, Rosemond W. Purcell, Susan Moldenhauer, and Carolyn Chute. At the Cleveland Institute of Art my first teacher of photography was Robert L. Palmer. For twenty years now I have benefitted from his guidance, assistance, and friendship.

At a time before any recognition for my work was achieved, one person had the courage and foresight to give his support. My deepest appreciation goes to Ray A. Graham III of the Elizabeth Firestone Graham Foundation. For his help in bringing a wider audience to my work I thank Allan Albert, President of the OPSIS Foundation, whose support has been invaluable. In the making of the actual photographs I have for five years been a recipient of the Polaroid Corporation's Artist Materials Support Grant. This program is essential for the making of certain photographs. My special thanks go to Barbara Hitchcock and Linda Benedict-Jones of the Polaroid Corporation.

I am grateful to Salem State College for a year's sabbatical leave from my teaching position to work on this project and to the National Endowment for the Arts for a photography fellowship that enabled me to complete the work for this book.

My appreciation goes to Lee Smith for giving voices to my photographs, to JoAnne Prichard, my editor at the University Press of Mississippi for believing in my work as a book, and to John Langston at the press for his excellent layout and design of this book.

WORK IN PERMANENT COLLECTIONS

International Center of Photography, New York, NY
Los Angeles County Museum of Art, Los Angeles, CA
San Francisco Museum of Modern Art, San Francisco, CA
The Museum of Fine Arts, Houston, TX
Center for Creative Photography, Tucson, AZ
Harvard University, Cambridge, MA
Polaroid Collection, Cambridge, MA
Museum of Photographic Arts, San Diego, CA
New Orleans Museum of Art, New Orleans, LA
University of Kentucky, Lexington, KY
Bayly Art Museum, University of Virginia, Charlottesville, VA
Cincinnati Art Museum, Cincinnati, OH
Cleveland Museum of Art, Cleveland, OH
University of New Mexico, University Art Museum, Albuquerque, NM
Corcoran Gallery of Art, Washington, DC
Museum of Modern Art, New York, NY
National Museum of American Art, Smithsonian Institute, Washington, DC

Library of Congress Cataloging-in-Publication Data

Adams, Shelby Lee.

Appalachian portraits / photographs by Shelby Lee Adams ;
narrative by Lee Smith.
p. cm. — (Author and artist series)
ISBN 0-87805-646-7 (cloth). — ISBN 0-87805-667-X (paper)
1. Appalachian Region, Southern—Social life and customs.
2. Appalachian Region, Southern—Pictorial works. 3. Kentucky—
Social life and customs. 4. Kentucky—Pictorial works. 5. Napier
family. 6. Sloan family. 7. Appalachian Region, Southern—
-Biography—Portraits. 8. Kentucky—Biography—Portraits.
I. Smith, Lee. II. Title. III. Series.
F217. A65A23 1993
974—dc20 93-4688
CIP